THE TEMPEST

EDITED BY

FREDERICK S. BOAS, M.A.

INSPECTOR IN ENGLISH TO THE L.C.C. EDUCATION DEPARTMENT
SOMETIME EXHIBITIONER OF BALLIOL COLLEGE, OXFORD
AUTHOR OF "SHAKSPERE AND HIS PREDECESSORS"

BLACKIE & SON LIMITED
LONDON AND GLASGOW

BLACKIE & SON LIMITED
    50 Old Bailey, London
    17 Stanhope Street, Glasgow

BLACKIE & SON (INDIA) LIMITED
    Warwick House, Fort Street, Bombay

BLACKIE & SON (CANADA) LIMITED
                Toronto

Printed in Great Britain by Blackie & Son, Ltd., Glasgow

GENERAL PREFACE

In this edition of SHAKESPEARE an attempt is made to present the greater plays of the dramatist in their literary aspect, and not merely as material for the study of philology or grammar. Criticism purely verbal and textual has only been included to such an extent as may serve to help the student in the appreciation of the essential poetry. Questions of date and literary history have been fully dealt with in the Introductions, but the larger space has been devoted to the interpretative rather than the matter-of-fact order of scholarship. Aesthetic judgments are never final, but the Editors have attempted to suggest points of view from which the analysis of dramatic motive and dramatic character may be profitably undertaken. In the Notes likewise, while it is hoped that all unfamiliar expressions and allusions have been adequately explained, yet it has been thought even more important to consider the dramatic value of each scene, and the part which it plays in relation to the whole. These general principles are common to the whole series; in detail each Editor is alone responsible for the play intrusted to him.

Every volume of the series has been provided with a Glossary, an Essay upon Metre, and an Index; and Appendices have been added upon points of special interest, which could not conveniently be treated in the Introduction or the Notes. The text is based by the several Editors on that of the *Globe* edition: the only omissions made are those that are unavoidable in an edition likely to be used by young students.

By the systematic arrangement of the introductory matter, and by close attention to typographical details, every effort has been made to provide an edition that will prove convenient in use.

THE WARWICK SHAKESPEARE. General editor, Professor C. H. HERFORD, Litt.D., F.B.A.

Play	Edited by
ANTONY AND CLEOPATRA.	A. E. Morgan, M.A., and W. Sherard Vines, M.A.
AS YOU LIKE IT	J. C. Smith, M.A., B.A.
CORIOLANUS.	Sir Edmund K. Chambers, K.B.E., C.B., M.A.. D.Litt.
CYMBELINE.	A. J. Wyatt, M.A.
HAMLET.	Sir Edmund K. Chambers.
HENRY THE FOURTH—Part I.	F. W. Moorman, B.A., Ph.D.
HENRY THE FOURTH—Part II.	C. H. Herford, Litt.D., F.B.A.
HENRY THE FIFTH.	G. C. Moore Smith, D.Litt., Ph.D., LL.D.
HENRY THE EIGHTH.	D. Nichol Smith, M.A., D.Litt.
JULIUS CÆSAR.	Arthur D. Innes, M.A.
KING JOHN.	G. C. Moore Smith.
KING LEAR.	D. Nichol Smith.
LOVE'S LABOUR'S LOST.	A. E. Morgan, M.A., and W. Sherard Vines, M.A.
MACBETH.	Sir Edmund K. Chambers.
THE MERCHANT OF VENICE.	H. L. Withers.
A MIDSUMMER-NIGHT'S DREAM.	Sir Edmund K. Chambers.
MUCH ADO ABOUT NOTHING.	J. C. Smith, M.A., B.A.
OTHELLO.	C. H. Herford, Litt.D., F.B.A.
RICHARD THE SECOND.	C. H. Herford.
RICHARD THE THIRD.	Sir George Macdonald, K.C.B., D.Litt., LL.D.
ROMEO AND JULIET	J. E. Crofts, B.Litt.
THE TEMPEST.	F. S. Boas, M.A., LL.D.
TROILUS AND CRESSIDA.	Bonamy Dobrée, O.B.E., M.A.
TWELFTH NIGHT.	Arthur D. Innes, M.A.
THE WINTER'S TALE.	C. H. Herford.

CONTENTS

ADDENDUM: SHAKESPEARE'S STAGE IN ITS BEARING UPON HIS DRAMA, by Prof. C. H. HERFORD, Litt.D.

INTRODUCTION

I.—THE DATE OF THE PLAY

§ 1. The date of *The Tempest* is one of the most vexed problems of Shakespearean criticism, and cannot be fixed with
complete certainty. The play was printed for the   First Edition,
first time, as far as we know, in the collected   1623.
edition of Shakespeare's works, 1623, known as the First
Folio. Thus all conclusions as to its date must be based
upon internal evidence or conjectural allusions in contemporary writings.

§ 2. Hunter, in his *Disquisition on the Scene, Origin, Date,
&c., of Shakespeare's Tempest* (1839), assigned the play to
the spring or summer of 1596. He identified it   Hunter's con-
with *Love's Labour's Won* mentioned by Francis   jectural date,
Meres in his list of twelve of Shakespeare's plays   1596.
(1598), and considered that its references to travellers' tales
were inspired by Raleigh's narrative of his Voyage to Guiana
(1596). Hunter assumed further that Ben Jonson, in the Prologue to *Every Man in his Humour*[1], was alluding to *The
Tempest* in the following lines:

> " He rather prays you will be pleased to see
> One such to-day, as other plays should be;
> Where neither chorus wafts you o'er the seas
> Nor creaking throne comes down the boys to please;
> *Nor nimble squib is seen to make afeard*
> *The gentlewoman; nor roll'd bullet heard*

---

[1] We know of no performance of *Every Man in his Humour* before 1598, but
Hunter without warrant identified it with *The Umers* mentioned in Henslowe's
Diary, Nov. 25, 1596.

> *To say, it thunders: nor tempestuous drum*
> *Rumbles, to tell you when the storm doth come.*
> .   .   .   *There's hope left then,*
> *You, that have so grac'd monsters may like men."*

In the italicised lines Hunter detected references to (1) the descent of Juno in the Masque in Act iv.; (2) the thunder and lightning in Act i. Sc. 1; (3) the monster Caliban. But the allusions are very doubtful, and, in any case, they give no support to Hunter's theory. For this Prologue does not appear in the quarto edition, 1601, of *Every Man in his Humour*, and is first found in the folio edition of Ben Jonson's works, 1616. Apart from this, however, and from the evidences treated below, one fact is fatal to Hunter's hypothesis. Gonzalo's sketch of his ideal commonwealth (ii. 1. 141–158) is borrowed almost verbally from Florio's translation of Montaigne, of which no printed edition is known before 1603, and which, from a statement of Florio himself, cannot have been begun till after 1599.

§ 3. This debt of the dramatist to Montaigne forms the starting-point of the German critic Elze's theory, which assigns the play to 1604. Ben Jonson, in his *Volpone* (iii. 2), 1605, alludes to thefts by English authors from the French essayist. As Gonzalo's speech is the principal passage in extant Elizabethan literature taken from Montaigne, Elze concludes that the sarcastic reference is to *The Tempest*, which he accordingly places in the year between the publication of Florio's version and the production of *Volpone*. But the allusion is too vague to be thus pressed, nor does it gain much support from Elze's second argument that Shakespeare was also indebted to *Darius*, a tragedy by the Earl of Stirling, 1603, which contains (iv. 2) these lines:

Elze's conjectural date, 1604.

> " Let greatness of her glascie scepters vaunt;
> Not sceptours, no, but reeds, soone bruis'd soone broken:
> And let this worldlie pomp our wits inchant.
> All fades, and scarcelie leaues behind a token.
> Those golden Pallaces, those gorgeous halles,

With fourniture superfluouslie faire:
　Those statelie courts, those sky-encountring walles
Evanish all like vapours in the aire."

There is an undoubted similarity between these verses and
Prospero's words (iv. 1) beginning "And, like this insubstantial pageant faded", but the parallel may simply have
been accidental, as the transitoriness of earthly magnificence
is a commonplace of thought, and even if Shakespeare had
read Stirling's lines they might easily have found an echo in
his verse later than 1604.

§ 4. The safer way to ascertain the approximate date of *The
Tempest* is to set aside these highly conjectural inferences in
favour of indisputable evidence afforded by the　　Internal
metre, *style*, and *spirit* of the play. Shakespeare's　evidence.
metrical practice underwent great changes dur-　　1. Metre.
ing his career as playwright. (*a*) Rhyme diminishes from
Love's Labour's Lost, where it occurs in 62 verses in every
100, to *The Winter's Tale*, where it is entirely absent: in *The
Tempest* there is one rhyming couplet. (*b*) Double endings
tend to increase, though not uniformly; they are fewest in
1 Henry IV., where they are 8 per cent, and most numerous in
The Tempest, 35 per cent. (*c*) *Enjambements* or run-on lines
increase from 8 per cent in *The Taming of the Shrew* to 46
per cent in *Cymbeline*: in *The Tempest* they are 41 per cent.
(*d*) Speech-endings not coincident with verse-endings increase
from *1 Henry VI.*, ½ per cent, to *Winter's Tale*, 87 per cent:
in *The Tempest* there are 84 per cent.[1] By the first test *The
Tempest* stands last but one among the plays; by the second
it stands last; by the third, last but three; by the fourth, last
but two. The combined evidence of these tests assigns the
play, beyond doubt, to Shakespeare's final period, between
about 1608 and 1613.

§ 5. The evidence of *style* supports this conclusion. In
Shakespeare's youthful works thought often lags
behind power of expression, and we thus find　　2. Style.
thin, laboured, and rhetorical passages. In the dramatist's

---

[1] The figures are taken from G. König's *Der Vers in Shakspeare's Dramen*.

central period, from about 1597 to 1606, thought and expression attain to an exquisite balance, and it is during these years that Shakespeare produces his most flawless work. But afterwards his wealth of ideas tends to outgrow the capacity of his instrument, and the result is a style elliptical to a fault, and overriding the canons of syntax observed in earlier plays. Of this style in its fullest development *The Tempest* is throughout an example.

§ 6. The *spirit* of the play and the nature of its incidents also assign it to Shakespeare's last years. From about 1600 to 1608 he put forth, probably under the stimulus of personal grief, his great series of tragedies. But afterwards his mood underwent a change, accompanied by a change in his choice of materials. Romantic themes henceforth engaged his pen—tales of kindred parted by wrongdoing or misadventure, and reunited after many years. Reconciliation and repentance are the keynotes of this closing group of dramas, and in *The Tempest* they are struck in the clearest tones.

3. Spirit.

§ 7. Thus these converging lines of *internal* evidence forbid us to place the play earlier than 1608. On the other hand, it was well known by 1614, as is plain from the Induction to *Bartholomew Fair*, where Ben Jonson uses these words : " If there be never a *Servant-monster* i' the Fayre who can helpe it, he says ; nor a nest of *Antiques* ? He is loth to make Nature afraid in his Playes, like those that beget *Tales, Tempests*, and such like *Drolleries*." The italicised phrases refer, beyond reasonable doubt, to *The Tempest* and *The Winter's Tale*, which are mentioned in the Vertue *MSS.* as having been performed with twelve others on the 20th May, 1613, before the Elector Palatine and Princess Elizabeth, the daughter of King James. Dr. Garnett[1], trusting to the authority of this *MSS.*, concludes that *The Tempest* was written for their marriage, which took place 14th February, 1613. The introduction (in Act iii.) of the bridal-masque, which has so little connection with the main plot, raises the strongest presumption that the piece was

Dr. Garnett dates the play 1613.

----

[1] *Universal Review*, April, 1889.

composed in honour of a wedding, and Dr. Garnett argues that everything corresponds with the royal marriage of 1613. "The foreign prince come from beyond sea, the island princess who has never left her home, the wise father who brings about the auspicious consummation by his policy; all found their counterparts among the splendid company that watched the performance on that February night." Dr. Garnett further sees in the story of Prince Ferdinand an exquisitely skilful allusion to the sudden death of Prince Henry in November, 1612, during the progress of the marriage negotiations. "The recent calamity is not unrecognised; on the contrary, the supposed death of the drowned Prince is a most vital incident, kept continually in view. But by a consummate stroke of genius, the woe is taken from Prospero, the representative of James, and transferred to the house of his enemy. The lost prince is duly mourned, but not by his real father. James is reminded of his bereavement, but it is not obtruded on him. In the end the hitherto sonless Prospero gains a son, as the bereaved James is gaining one in the Palatine."

§ 8. Dr. Garnett's theory is suggestively worked out, and the date for which he contends is not impossible. But the metrical evidence is not in favour of *The Tempest* being two years later than *The Winter's Tale*, which was seen at the Globe Theatre on May 15, 1611, by Dr. Forman. The two plays seem rather to have been written almost at the same time, and the internal tests thus support Malone's suggestion that *The Tempest* was inspired in part Probable date, 1610-11. by Silvester Jourdan's narrative of the wreck of Sir George Somers' ship, *The Sea-Venture*, off the Bermudas. The wreck took place in July, 1609, and during the latter part of that year much anxiety was felt for the fate of the crew, as is proved by the issue of a pamphlet by the Council of Virginia to allay apprehension. After the safe return of the ship-wrecked company to England, Jourdan, who was one of their number, published his account, dated 13th October, 1610. The parallel points between his tract and *The Tempest* are discussed in III. § 13, and they suggest the end of 1610 or the beginning of 1611 as the date of the play. But resemblances still more striking exist between the piece and another account of the wreck by William Strachey. If Strachey's pamphlet, as there is ground for supposing, was not printed till 1612, this would favour Garnett's hypothesis of 1613 being the date. But the matter is too uncertain to outweigh the metrical tests, and to sum up, we may assert that *The Tempest* certainly belongs to Shakespeare's final period, that it probably dates from 1610–11, but that possibly it may be as late as 1612–13.

II.—LITERARY HISTORY

§ 9. *The Tempest* is the opening play in the Folio of 1623, and the text is of remarkable purity. It shares with *The Two Gentlemen of Verona* the distinction of being printed with more correctness than perhaps any other play in that volume. It is the shortest of Shakespeare's dramas except *The Comedy of Errors*, and contains 2064 lines. This exceptional brevity supports the view that it was originally composed for some Court entertainment. Some critics (*e.g.* Fleay and Grant-White) have conjectured that it has come down to us in a form abbreviated for this purpose; but it must be remembered that the play with its songs and dances, and elaborate masque in Act IV., would take longer in representation than the number of lines suggests.

§ 10. In spite of Ben Jonson's sarcasm, *The Tempest* was evidently from the first a popular play, and was imitated by succeeding dramatists, as Dryden testifies. "It had formerly been acted with success in the Black-Fryers: and our excellent Fletcher had so great a value for it, that he thought fit to make use of the same design, not much varied, a second time. Those who have seen his *Sea Voyage* may easily discern that it was a copy of Shakespeare's *Tempest*: the Storm, the Desart Island, and the Woman who had never seen a Man, are all sufficient testimonies of it. But Fletcher was not the only poet who made use of Shakespeare's plot: Sir John Suckling, a professed admirer of our author, has followed his footsteps in his *Goblins*, his *Regmella* being an open imitation of Shakespeare's *Miranda*; and his Spirits, though counterfeit, yet are copied from *Ariel*." These words are taken from Dryden's preface[1] to his own and Davenant's version of the play, *The Enchanted Island*, produced at the Duke of York's Theatre in 1667, and published in 1670. The original suggestion of this version came, as Dryden acknowledges, from Davenant; the added scenes, as the German essayist Grimm has shown, are translated from a drama by the Spanish writer, Calderon.

Dryden and Davenant's Enchanted Island, 1667.

In this Restoration version the play is robbed of more than half its poetry; and of all its moral elevation and exquisite purity of tone. Yet it would be unfair to deny that *The Enchanted Island* is a very deft piece of craftsmanship, and, measured by the artistic and moral standard of its day, must be pronounced a success. The somewhat tedious plot of Sebastian and Antonio against Alonso is omitted, as also the conspiracy of Caliban and his allies against Prospero. Instead we have an amusing political burlesque. Stephano elects himself Duke, with Mustacho the mate, and Ventoso, a mariner, as Vice-Roys, but Trincalo *(sic)* sets up an opposition *régime*, supported by Caliban and his sister Sycorax, whom he makes his bride. The desire to share Trincalo's butt of wine makes Stephano's party submit to the rival rule, but after a joint-potation discord breaks out again. All this is excellent fooling, which would be specially appreciated by spectators who had passed through the troubled period of the Civil War and Commonwealth. But the figure of Caliban is shorn of the features that clothe it with a wild poetry and dignity, and Ariel is vulgarized by being represented in love with another spirit, Milcha.

In the main plot Miranda has associated with her a sister, Dorinda, while dwelling in another part of the cave is Hippolito, rightful heir to the dukedom of Mantua. Bequeathed in infancy to Prospero's care, he has shared his fortunes, and is kept thus secluded because his horoscope portends death should he see the face of woman. His

---

[1] This preface is given in full in Appendix A.

chance encounter with Dorinda, and their love at first sight, followed by the similar passion between Miranda and the shipwrecked Ferdinand; the duel between the princes because Hippolito claims the right to love all women; the apparent death of Hippolito and his restoration by Ariel's balms; the attendant entanglements that ensue for a time—all this makes up a plot far-fetched and often disagreeably suggestive, but, unfolded in easy and fluent dialogue, very effective for stage purposes. The opportunities for spectacular effect, in which the original play had been so rich, were yet further multiplied in the revised version. The Masque of Iris, Ceres, and Juno is left out, but instead we have one of devils and personified sins, which appears to Alonso and his companions, and another of the Sea-Deities, which closes the play. The success of this Restoration version is clear from repeated entries in Pepys' diary. Thus on November 7, 1667, Pepys writes: "At noon resolved with Sir W. Pen to go to see *The Tempest*, an old play of Shakespeare's, acted I hear the first day. . . The house mighty full; the King and Court there ; and the most innocent play that ever I saw. The play has no great wit, but yet good, above ordinary plays." A week later the diarist's verdict was more enthusiastic : "Saw *The Tempest* again, which is very pleasant, and full of so good variety that I cannot be more pleased almost in a comedy, only the seamen's part a little too tedious". And four more visits testify to Pepys' appreciation of the play, and to its hold on the Restoration public.

§ 11. In later days *The Tempest's* magnetic influence has inspired independent works which seek to develop certain of its aspects. *The Virgin Queen*, by F. G. Waldron, 1797, is a melodramatic production narrating the additional dangers which Prospero and his relatives endure on the return journey to Milan, and from which they are only delivered when Ariel restores to Prospero his drowned book and buried staff.

Waldron's
Virgin Queen,
1797.

On a very different plane is Ernest Renan's *Caliban*[1], a

---

[1] For a detailed analysis of Renan's *Caliban*, see Furness' *Variorum* edition of *The Tempest*, 383–386.

dramatized piece of political philosophy. The scene is laid at Milan after Prospero's return, and deals with Renan's
Caliban. a second successful revolt of Caliban, who represents the spirit of modern social democracy, viewed by unfriendly eyes. By working on the greed and discontent of the multitude Caliban supplants Prospero, who finds that his charms are of no avail against a generation that has lost its belief in the supernatural. Once enthroned, however, Caliban realizes that he is an Institution, and prepares to protect himself. He sees that Prospero, representing Art and Philosophy, may be useful in his service, and so refuses to give him up to the Inquisition, representing Clericalism, which wishes to prosecute him for sorcery. "His works will be the glory of my reign. I shall have my share in them. I exploit him; 't is the law of the world."

It is under a different aspect that Caliban is viewed in Browning's powerful poem, *Caliban upon Setebos*. The untutored intelligence of the savage (who, with his Browning's
Caliban upon
Setebos. rudimentary sense of personality, speaks of himself in the third person) is groping among the mysteries of existence—the problem of pain, the apparently capricious government of the world, and the nature of the Being who is responsible for it. He conceives of Setebos, his dam's god, as a creature after his own likeness, cruel, cunning, and full of purposeless malignity, whose anger can be best evaded by a pretence of being miserable. Above Setebos he dimly imagines a higher power, Quiet, without joy or grief, and his hope is that Quiet may conquer Setebos, or that the latter may grow old and doze, which would be as good as if He were dead. But at this moment the bursting of a terrible storm warns him that his speculations have been overheard, and he grovels in an agony of fear.

> "White blaze—
> A tree's head snaps—and there, there there, there there,
> His thunder follows! Fool to gibe at Him!
> So! 'Lieth flat and loveth Setebos."

§ 12. Musicians also have found *The Tempest* a fertile source of inspiration. Thirteen of its passages have been used as the *libretto* for songs. Two of the settings, to "Full fadom five", i. 2. 396-404, and "Where the bee sucks", v. i. 88-94, were, there is reason to believe, used in Shakespeare's own time. They are given in Wilson's *Cheerful Ayres or Ballads*, 1660, with the name of the composer, R. Johnson. This Johnson, after being in the service of Sir T. Kytson, came to London and composed music for plays, including Middleton's *Witch* and Shakespeare's *Tempest*.

III.—THE SOURCE OF THE INCIDENTS

§ 13. The source of *The Tempest*, like the date, cannot be definitely ascertained. But in both cases an investigation of the subject is amply repaid by the interesting and suggestive issues raised. Mention has been made above (§ 8) of Jourdan's pamphlet, *A Discovery of the Barmudas*. He relates that the crew of *The Sea-Venture*, weary with pumping, had "given up all for lost, and *begun to take leave of each other*, intending to commit themselves to the mercy of the sea", when Sir George Somers at length descried land and encouraged them—*many from weariness having fallen asleep* —to continue at the pumps. They complied, and fortunately "the ship was driven and *jammed between two rocks*, fast lodged and locked for further budging". One hundred and fifty persons got ashore, and as Jourdan continues, "our provision was beyond our hopes . . . most admirable; for this Islands of the Bermudas . . . were *never inhabited* by any Christian or heathen people, but ever esteemed and reputed *a most prodigious and inchanted place*, affording nothing but gusts, storms, and foul weather. . . . Yet did we find there *the ayre . . . temperate* and *the country abundantly fruitfull*." The italicised phrases, if compared with i. 1. 58; i. 2. 232; v. 1. 230; ii. 2. 54; ii. 1. 34-50, show a similarity that can scarcely be accidental. Even more remarkable are some of the expressions used in Strachey's narrative of the same shipwreck. "Upon the

Thursday night Sir George Summers being upon the watch had an apparition of a little round light, like a faint star, trembling and streaming along with a sparkling blaze, half the height upon the main-mast, and shooting sometimes from shroud to shroud, tempting to settle as it were upon any of the four shrouds. . . . We threw overboard much luggage . . . and stowed many a butt of beer, hogsheads of oil, cider, wine, and vinegar." . . . On the island "some dangerous and discontents nourished amongst us had like to have been the parents of bloody issues and mischiefs". Do we not seem to have here the suggestions for Ariel's apparition on the topmast, in the form of flame, for Stephano's escape upon a butt of sack which the sailors heaved o'erboard, and for the conspiracy of Antonio and Sebastian against Alonso?[1]

§ 14. But it is a misconception into which some critics have fallen, to think that Shakespeare actually lays the scene of the play in the Bermudas. On the contrary, Ariel (i. 2. 229) speaks of fetching dew *from* "the still-vext Bermoothes", though the allusion proves that the locality was prominently in Shakespeare's thoughts at the time. Hunter ingeniously seeks to identify Prospero's island with Lampedusa, off the north coast of Africa. His main argument is that the island's geographical position would meet all the exigencies of the story; sailors from Algiers would conveniently and naturally land Sycorax on its shores; Prospero, if committed to the sea off an Italian coast, and tossed by winds and waves, would most likely drift to Lampedusa; and Alonso, sailing from Tunis and steering for Naples, would be caught in the storm raised by Prospero and landed there. Moreover, Lampedusa was noted as stormy, it had the reputation of being haunted, and contained caves and a hermit's cell. Elze has made out an equally detailed case in favour of another Mediterranean islet, Pantalaria; and a third critic states dogmatically that

The Bermudas not the scene of the play.

Hunter's identification of the island with Lampedusa.

---

[1] In any case no weight can be attached to Hunter's theory that the description of the storm (i. 1) was borrowed from Canto 41 of Harrington's translation of Ariosto's *Orlando Furioso*.

it could only have been Corcyra which was intended. But they who thus seek to bring the enchanted island within the sphere of workaday geography imagine a vain thing: it is not to be found on charts or maps, but floats, "east of the sun, west of the moon", washed by

> "the foam
> Of perilous seas in faery lands forlorn".

§ 15. If geography is thus silent as to the whereabouts of the mysterious island, history enlightens us almost equally little about the Italian potentates who are drifted to its shores. But it is noteworthy that some of the names and incidents introduced into *The Tempest* occur in Thomas' *Historye of Italye*, 1561. We there read that *Prospero* Adorno was established as the Duke of Millain's lieutenant in Genoa, 1477; "but he continued scarcely one year, till by mean of new practices that he held with *Ferdinando*, King of Naples, he was had in suspicion to the Milanese". He was deposed, and *Antony* Adorno was made governor of the city instead. Thomas further relates that there was an Alonzo, King of Naples, whose son, Ferdinand, succeeded him in 1495. This Alonzo united the houses of Naples and Milan by marrying a princess of the latter city. In the play this incident is transferred to his son.

Slender historical framework.

§ 16. But the sources hitherto spoken of can, in any case, have only supplied the dramatist with the framework of his plot, and do not account for the central incidents of the story. Collins, the poet, told Warton that they were derived from a romance, *Aurelio and Isabella*, printed in Italian, Spanish, French, and English in 1588, but there is really no connection between this novel and the play. More fruitful was Tieck's discovery in 1817 of some remarkable points of resemblance between *The Tempest* and *Die Schöne Sidea* (*The Fair Sidea*), by Jacob Ayrer, a notary in Nürnberg. Ayrer, who rose from humble circumstances to an official position, died in 1605, and in 1618 a folio edition of his dramas was published with the title, *Opus Theatricum.*

Ayrer's Die Schöne Sidea.

Die Schöne Sidea,[1] one of the pieces in this volume, tells the story of a Duke Ludolff of Lithuania and his daughter Sidea. Ludolff is dethroned, and expelled from his kingdom with Sidea, by Prince Leudegast of Wiltau. He takes refuge in a wood, and by his magic arts, and the aid of a devil, Runcifal, gets into his possession Leudegast's son, Engelbrecht, who has lost his way while hunting. Engelbrecht and his squire try to draw their swords to defend themselves, but find that their weapons are charmed from moving. Engelbrecht is then taken prisoner, and set to bear logs for Sidea, who at first treats him as harshly as her father. But his noble birth and beauty win her heart, and they fly together. After sundry adventures, in which for a time they are separated, they reach Leudegast's court, and the piece ends with their marriage, and the reconciliation of the two princes. Intermingled with this main plot are episodes of low comedy which have no relation to the humorous scenes in *The Tempest*, and throughout the German and the English plays the names of persons and localities are entirely different. But this does not affect the striking parallelism between the central situations in the two dramas. In both there is a deposed ruler, expelled with his daughter as sole companion, and practising in banishment the magic art; in both he gets into his power his enemy's son, whose sword he has enchanted, and whom he condemns to the task of log-bearing; in both the heroine and the captive prince fall in love, and the story closes with their marriage, and the reconcilation of their parents. There can be no reasonable doubt that either Shakespeare and Ayrer borrowed from a common source, or that the Englishman had a version of the Nürnberg play before him. The latter is far from unlikely, for we know that English actors were in Nürnberg in 1604 and 1606, and that in June, 1613, the Elector of Brandenburg's servants and the English comedians acted several "beautiful comedies and tragedies" including a "Sedea", which can scarcely have been any other

---

[1] A full prose translation of Ayrer's play is given by Furness in his *Variorum* edition of *The Tempest*, 326–341. A verse translation is given by Cohn, *Shakespeare in Germany*.

than Ayrer's play. When English companies were so frequently visiting Nürnberg, what more likely than that they
should bring home versions of some of Ayrer's favourite
pieces, and that one of these should fall into Shakespeare's
hands?

§ 17. Other works to which *The Tempest* is indebted in a
minor degree, *e.g.* Florio's *Montaigne*, Golding's *Ovid*, and
Eden's *History of Travayle*, are referred to in the notes. But
there is another probable source, different in kind from those
Prospero and   spoken of, which claims a word.   Does *The*
Shakespeare.   *Tempest* reflect symbolically the circumstances
of Shakespeare's own career at the period of its composition?
To this question a strongly affirmative answer has been given
by writers like Emile Montégut, who asserts[1] that it is
"clearly the last of Shakespeare's dramas, and, under the
form of an allegory, is the dramatic last will and testament
of the great poet". The statement made in this unqualified
form overshoots the mark, for *The Tempest* is very probably
not Shakespeare's last complete play, and certainly not the
last in which he had a share. Yet the world is assuredly
right in its instinct that the voice of Prospero is, in peculiar
measure, the voice of Shakespeare, and that when the great
enchanter, at whose command "graves have waked their
sleepers", abjures his magic, the great dramatist is in some
sort bidding a farewell, though scarcely formal and final, to
the theatre, where his "potent art" had resummoned the
mighty dead to new and imperishable life.[2]

IV.—CRITICAL APPRECIATION

§ 18. The popularity enjoyed by *The Tempest* from the time
of its production is the more remarkable because the play
lacks some of the customary elements of dramatic interest.
The plot is comparatively slight, and, as we know from the

---

[1] *Revue des Deux Mondes*, 1865.
[2] See further the passage in Dowden's *Shakespeare's Mind and Art*, referred
to in Appendix B.

first that Prospero has absolute control over the development
of events, we are never stirred by the feeling of
suspense which keeps the attention keenly alert — Dramatic elements
during the progress of a piece. Nor is the play — absent in *The Tempest*.
as rich as many others in studies of human
character. The principal personages belong to the world of
romance, and are either in part or entirely outside the pale of
ordinary experience, while the subordinate figures have no
strongly-marked individuality and are little more than types.
Nor does Shakespeare's humorous genius show to full
advantage. The buffoonery of Stephano and Trinculo has
a large element of mere horse-play, and even the earliest
comedies scarcely contain passages of such wire-drawn, in-
sipid repartee as make up the main part of Act ii. sc. i.[1]

§ 19. How is it that, nevertheless, *The Tempest* ranks among
the most fascinating, if not, strictly speaking, the greatest of
Shakespeare's plays?   In the first place, as we have seen, it
appeals more than any other play except *Hamlet* to that per-
manent instinct which craves to catch a glimpse of William
Shakespeare's own personality through and behind his cre-
ations.   Yet at the same time the piece transports us to
regions strangely remote from the Globe Theatre
or the Avon's banks. Throughout it we hear — Echoes in *The Tempest* of Elizabethan adventure.
echoes of the wonderful adventures of the
Elizabethan seamen, of the discoveries and
"plantations" wherewith the expansion of England began.
As we read of the "mountaineers dew-lapped like bulls", and
the "men whose heads stood in their breasts"; or of the
"putters-out of five" and the "holiday fools" eager to lay out
ten doits to see a dead Indian or a painted monster, we call
up a picture of Frobisher and Davis' voyages in search of the
north-west passage, of Raleigh's exploration of Guiana, of
Drake's journey round the world. We seem to stand on the
quay of some old-world Cornish or Devonshire seaport, and
to form a part of the open-mouthed crowd listening to the
tales of bronzed mariners, and staring at the treasures that

[1] This has, however, a partial dramatic justification. See the introduction to
the scene in the *Notes*.

they have brought from Eldorados far away. No other work of Shakespeare reflects so vividly this enthralling aspect of Elizabethan life, and this is a main secret of its charm.

§ 20. But *The Tempest* transports us not only to new-found regions over seas, but to poetic wonderlands undiscoverable by the most adventurous of voyagers. The distinction, however, in that age of geographical marvels was less well defined than to-day, and Shakespeare, if questioned as to the where-abouts of the uninhabited island, might well have answered in the semi-serious vein of Spenser's Introduction to Book II. of *The Faerie Queene*—

The super-natural in *The Tempest*.

> "Who ever heard of the Indian Peru?
> Or who in venturous vessel measured
> The Amazons' huge river, now found trew?
> Or fruitfullest Virginia who did ever view?
>
> Yet all these were, when no man did them know;
> Yet have from wisest ages hidden beene;
> And later times things more unknowne shall show.
> Why then should witlesse man so much misweene
> That nothing is, but that which he hath seene?"

It is in an age when the borderlands of the natural and the supernatural thus overlap that the creative artist can most unerringly give to the latter the "form and pressure" of reality. Prospero's kingdom, the island,

> "Full of noises,
> Sounds and sweet airs, that give delight and hurt not",

has as unquestionable an existence for us as if it were marked on every map of the southern seas. But it is characteristic of Shakespeare that he shows a wise economy in his use of supernatural effects, and, as a rule restricts their display to a limited time and area. In *A Midsummer-Night's Dream* the fairies are seen exercising their powers of enchantment only within the haunted wood, and for a single night. Similarly in *The Tempest* we witness the operation of Prospero's omnipotent art for the short space of three hours, and not

beyond the confines of the mysterious isle. Hence in form
the work has many of the characteristics of a Classical play.
It preserves the Unities of time, and, in essentials, of place;
and Act i. sc. 2, as far as line 375, is practically equivalent
to the Classical Prologue which enlightens the audience on
preceding events necessary to the understanding of the
action. In its closely-knit structure *The Tempest* forms the
strongest contrast to *The Winter's Tale* and *Pericles*, which,
with kindred incidents, exhibit the license of the Romantic
type in its extreme form.

§ 21. Of the majority of the spirits with which the island is
thronged, and which form its original inhabitants, we only
get passing glimpses, as in Prospero's final invocation:

> "Ye elves of hills, brooks, standing lakes and groves,
>   And ye that on the sands with printless foot
>   Do chase the ebbing Neptune and do fly him
>   When he comes back; you demi-puppets that
>   By moonshine do the green sour ringlets make,
>   Whereof the ewe not bites, and you whose pastime
>   Is to make midnight mushrooms, that rejoice
>   To hear the solemn curfew".

In Ariel's songs we catch echoes of the burthen of the
"sweet sprites", as they foot it featly on the yellow sands,
and of the "ding-dong" of the sea-nymphs as they ring the
knell of the drowned mariner. Other spirits we see performing varied services at Prospero's command. They invite strangers to partake of a banquet which vanishes in
thunder and lightning, they play the parts in a masque, or
in the shape of dogs hunt misdoers till they roar with
fright.

Akin to these "meaner ministers", but of loftier degree in
the elfin hierarchy, is Ariel. He had been imprisoned by
Sycorax, the mother of Caliban, for twelve years   Ariel.
in a cloven pine because he was

> "a spirit too delicate
> To act her earthy and abhorr'd commands".

From this thraldom he had been set free by Prospero, and his gratitude is shown by his willing service:

> "All hail, great master! grave sir, hail! I come
> To answer thy best pleasure; be't to fly,
> To swim, to dive into the fire, to ride
> On the curl'd clouds, to thy strong bidding task
> Ariel and all his quality".

As his name implies, he is a spirit of the air, though he has affinity too with the element of fire. "Like air and fire he can penetrate everywhere, treading the ooze of the salt deep, running upon the sharp wings of the north, doing business in the veins of earth when it is baked with frost. His natural speech is music or waves of air."[1] This music of Ariel's works strangely on all who hear it. As it creeps by Ferdinand on the waters, it allays their fury and his passion, and draws him to Prospero's cell. It wakes Gonzalo at the critical moment, when Sebastian and Antonio are threatening the King's life; it speaks through the elements to Alonso, and arouses remorse in his breast. But just because he is a spirit of the air, Ariel, though he is correspondent to command, finds all human service galling, and begs for his liberty. The announcement that it is at hand makes him burst into a jubilant carol, and in the closing words of the play we see him dismissed to his natural haunts.

At the opposite scale of being is Caliban, son of the devil, and the witch, Sycorax. This "freckled whelp" not honoured with a human shape is allied to the grosser natural forces, and is contemptuously hailed as "thou earth", "thou tortoise". In his outward appearance, probably owing to his long, finny arms, he must have had some resemblance to a fish, which Trinculo at first sight takes him to be. Not without reason has he been claimed as an unconscious anticipation of the evolutionary "missing link", for he typifies humanity scarcely, if at all, raised above the brute stage. His name is probably an anagram of Cannibal, and he represents the savage, seen in his naked

Caliban.

---

[1] Moulton, *Shakespeare as a Dramatic Artist*, p. 257.

deformity, not through a rose-coloured Arcadian or Utopian mist. For a while this creature had been "lord of the island", or as he proudly puts it, his own king. But his dynasty had been overthrown when a strange succession of events brought a new ruler to the lonely domain.

§ 22. Prospero, Duke of Milan, had abandoned the reins of government to his brother, Antonio, and given himself up entirely to secret studies. Antonio, ambitious of the ducal title as well as the power, had, with the aid of the King of Naples, deposed Prospero, and set him adrift with his infant child, Miranda. Borne by wind Prospero. and wave to the shores of the island, Prospero had begun life anew. His misfortunes had not been entirely unmerited, for in Shakespeare's eyes the primary duty of a ruler is to rule, not to retire into seclusion for religious or intellectual meditation. Thus it is that Henry VI. and the Duke in *Measure for Measure* bring disaster upon their realms, and likewise is it with Prospero. But in his case "sweet are the uses of adversity", and he learns to the full the lessons of exile. Stripped of temporal sway he still retains his precious books, whence he wrings the secrets of magic lore, and becomes an all-powerful enchanter. And it must be remembered that to an Elizabethan audience this would have seemed far from impossible. Wizards, like Dr. Dee, with their symbolic staff and mantle, were familiar personages at the time, and they figure frequently in the literature of the day. But either like Spenser's Archimago, they use their powers for wicked ends, or, like Marlowe's Faustus, for purely personal gratification. The noble originality of Shakespeare's conception lies in the fact that Prospero turns his art to entirely beneficent purposes, and to the practical illustration of his own lofty words:

> "the rarer action is
> In virtue than in vengeance".

Thus if we miss the aesthetic gratification which comes from the gradual resolution of suspense, we are compensated by the spectacle of an omnipotent force overruling the dramatic issues into correspondence with our conception of a righteous government of the world.

Thus Prospero frees Ariel from imprisonment, but imposes a term of service on him before he grants him full liberty. Thus too he seeks at first to educate Caliban, until the monster puts his lessons to evil use, and repays the enchanter's kindness by an attack on Miranda's honour. Thereupon follows his reduction to slavery, and though we realize the necessity of such treatment, Prospero perhaps appeals to us least powerfully when he is showering abuse and threats on the creature of whom he confesses,

> "We cannot miss him: he does make our fire,
> Fetch in our wood and serves in offices
> That profit us".

The degradation of the savage by the civilized man for his own purposes has been so frequent an episode in the history of colonization that we are apt to sympathize instinctively with the weaker side.

§ 23. But it is characteristic of Shakespeare's marvellous impartiality that while he remorselessly unveils all that is gross and brutal in Caliban, he does not picture him as a mere Yahoo. His speech is not without a rude eloquence, and in his description of the island and its products he shows a vein of untutored imagination. Moreover, the course of events provides him with a couple of foils, who prove that even barbarism surpasses a stunted caricature of civilization, and acquires a classical dignity through the comparison. The shipwrecked butler, Stephano, by the magic of his "celestial liquor", wins in a moment Caliban's complete allegiance, which Prospero's nobler gifts have failed to secure. Confident in the powers of this "brave god", Caliban enters into a conspiracy with him and his shipmate to overthrow Prospero's rule, and to secure "freedom" for himself. However nefarious his design, he pursues it with a concentration of purpose that puts to shame his worthless allies, who let themselves be lured from their object by the bait of some trumpery booty. And when

Caliban, Stephano, and Trinculo.

the plot is foiled, Caliban has enough natural acuteness to recognize his own blunder.

> " What a thrice-double ass
> Was I, to take this drunkard for a god
> And worship this dull fool !"

His promise to be wise hereafter and seek for grace, and Prospero's conditional offer of pardon, if he trim the cave handsomely, give us hope that there is no need to despair of even the servant-monster's future.

§ 24. But Prospero has to deal with more highly-placed and dangerous offenders than Caliban and his confederates. Fate puts his former wrongdoers at his mercy, and gives them at the same time an opportunity of showing whether they have repented of their misdeeds. Alonso, the King of Naples, agonized by the supposed loss of his son in the shipwreck, feels remorse stirring in his breast, and under the influence of Ariel's warnings bursts into fierce self-reproach. Antonio, the chief mover in the original crime, proves himself hardened in sin by the lapse of years. Even as Duke of Milan he has not been satisfied. He has found it galling to pay tribute to the King of Naples as his overlord, and in the shipwreck he spies an opportunity of getting rid of his burden. While Alonso, overcome with grief and fatigue, is sunk in sleep, he plans a treacherous attempt upon his life, with the aim of setting Sebastian on the Neapolitan throne, and freeing Milan from its pecuniary obligation. Prospero's vigilance frustrates the dastardly scheme, but the criminals are resolute to "take throughly" their next advantage at nightfall. Even Ariel's denunciation of their misdeeds, and his menace of "lingering perdition worse than any death" in default of repentance only rouse them to defiant rage. They dash with swords drawn after the vanishing "fiend", but their weapons avail them nothing, and the shipwrecked company are drawn by irresistible influence to the enchanter's cell.

Prospero cannot entirely conceal his inward tumult at this crisis. His nature, in spite of its stern schooling, has impassioned elements, and not only towards Caliban, but even towards Miranda and Ariel he betrays at times an intemperance of speech. Thus at the prospect of coming face to face with his enemies he is visibly agitated, and begs to be left alone. The conflict of emotions in his breast is sharp, but forgiveness triumphs over all lower feelings. "Prospero's forgiveness is solemn, judicial, and has in it something abstract and impersonal."[1] All sins are pardoned, yet a distinction is made among the sinners. Alonso, the least guilty and most repentant, is frankly welcomed; Antonio is sternly rebuked and bidden surrender the fruit of his misdeeds.

§ 25. Prospero exacts the restoration of his Dukedom, for so justice demands, but after his long exile he cares but little for the sweets of temporal sway, and in Milan his every third thought is to be his grave. It is less for his own sake than his daughter's that he claims again the royalties to which she is rightful heir. For if it falls to Prospero to pardon the guilty, it is also his prerogative to reward the innocent, and never maiden merited more entirely all that a father's love could bestow than Miranda.

Amidst the women drawn by Shakespeare she stands alone and apart. Mrs. Jameson has spoken of her as "the Eve of an enchanted Paradise", and the words are apt. For Miranda, reared among "the untrodden ways" of the tropical solitude, afar from the companionship of her own sex, is wanting in the complexity of character bred by artificial surroundings, and is a more ethereal type of womanhood in its primal innocence than Milton's picture of the mother of mankind.

Miranda.

Even in infancy she was a "cherubim" that did preserve her father in his strange adventure, and in her island-home she has been moulded by the "silent sympathy" of Nature's loveliness into peerless grace of body and mind. Caliban himself does homage to her beauty, and her exquisite tenderness and modesty shine through her every word and act. Her first utterance is one of pity for the shipwrecked crew:

[1] Dowden, *Shakespeare's Mind and Art.*

"O, I have suffered
With those that I saw suffer".

Prospero's story of their banishment does not draw from her
laments for her lost greatness, but sorrow at the thought of
the "trouble" she was then to him. But it is in her relations
with Ferdinand that the full charm of her nature is revealed.
So unlearned is she in worldly experience that when she first
looks on him she takes him for a spirit, and even when
Prospero assures her that "it eats and sleeps, and hath such
senses" as themselves, she declares:

"I might call him
A thing divine, for nothing natural
I ever saw so noble".

Nor is Ferdinand unworthy of this tribute. Though but
a man as other men are, he is a pattern hero of romance, a
model of high-bred gallantry. Between such a
pair love at first sight is inevitable, but Prospero   *Ferdinand.*
will not allow its course to run altogether smooth. He
brands the Prince as spy and traitor before Miranda's face,
and confines him in the cell. Ferdinand blithely accepts
bonds and drudgery, and proves that his is the true loyalty
that welcomes the meanest task when undergone for his
lady's sake. Theirs is indeed the rivalry of "two most rare
affections", for Miranda steals forth to help the Prince in his
task of log-bearing. But he declines the proffered aid; the
truly royal nature thinks no toil a burden in the sacred cause
of love:

"Hear my soul speak:
The very instant that I saw you, did
My heart fly to your service; there resides,
To make me slave to it; and for your sake
Am I this patient log-man".

And it is in a like spirit that Miranda tremblingly lays her
heart at her wooer's feet:

"I am your wife, if you will marry me;
If not, I'll die your maid: to be your fellow

> You may deny me; but I'll be your servant,
> Whether you will or no".

§ 26. Thus throughout *The Tempest*, giving unity to the varied scenes, runs the underlying conception that true freedom consists in service, in obedience to necessary social and moral laws. Prospero himself may be looked upon as exemplifying Bacon's dictum that man commands nature by obeying her. Symbolically he represents the true freedom of the scientific spirit, which by laboriously mastering the secret laws of the universe is able to turn them to its own purposes—in this case purposes of the highest beneficence. Against Prospero's rule, based on intellectual and moral supremacy, Caliban revolts. His is the perverted conception of 'freedom' which identifies it with unlimited license, and which kicks against all restraint. But life must be lived according to *some* law, and the being who rebels against the service of a Prospero is ready to do abject homage to a Stephano, in return for a few sips of liquor. Not different in spirit are the designs of Antonio, who, galled by his subordination to Prospero, and afterwards to Alonso, seeks by treachery and violence to free himself from the ties that bind him as brother and vassal. There is another more playful variation of the theme in Gonzalo's sketch of his ideal commonwealth, where the attempt to abolish all obligations between man and man results in hopeless contradiction. But not after methods such as these is freedom truly to be found. Miranda and Ferdinand, with the instinct of perfectly healthy natures, seek it by a far different road—that of loyal whole-hearted service and self-surrender in the bonds of mutual love. Ariel, too, puts "all his quality" gladly at Prospero's command, but he is a spirit, not to be permanently bound by human ties, and finding full liberty only in his own home of the elements.

Underlying idea of the play that freedom consists in service.

Implicit rather than directly emphasized, this idea of the paradoxical nature of freedom underlies the play, and gives it deeper significance than appears on the surface. And the thought finds its crowning illustration when Prospero, having accomplished his appointed work of punishment and pardon, bows himself again to human conditions, and of his own accord surrenders the omnipotence which he has only valued as the instrument of impersonal ends.

But it is not its "criticism of life" that gives *The Tempest* so secure a place in our affections. Its most powerful appeal is to that primary human instinct, which craves escape from the limiting conditions of the material universe, and joys to roam in the " ampler aether", the " diviner air" of poetic wonder-lands. In seasons when there is danger of the world being too much with us, it is an enfranchisement of the spirit to breathe the atmosphere of the enchanted island, and to have glimpses as fresh and pure as those for which the modern poet yearned when he was fain to

> " Have sight of Proteus rising from the sea,
> Or hear old Triton blow his wreathèd horn".

DRAMATIS PERSONÆ

ALONSO, King of Naples.

SEBASTIAN, his brother.

PROSPERO, the right Duke of Milan.

ANTONIO, his brother, the usurping Duke of Milan.

FERDINAND, son to the King of Naples.

GONZALO, an honest old Counsellor.

ADRIAN,
FRANCISCO, } Lords.

CALIBAN, a savage and deformed Slave.

TRINCULO, a Jester.

STEPHANO, a drunken Butler.

Master of a Ship.

Boatswain.

Mariners.

MIRANDA, daughter to Prospero.

ARIEL, an airy Spirit.

IRIS,
CERES,
JUNO, } presented by Spirits.
Nymphs,
Reapers,

Other Spirits attending on Prospero.

SCENE: *A ship at Sea: an island.*

THE TEMPEST

ACT I.

SCENE I. *On a ship at sea; a tempestuous noise of thunder and lightning heard.*

Enter a Ship-Master *and* a Boatswain.

Mast. Boatswain!

Boats. Here, master: what cheer?

Mast. Good, speak to the mariners: fall to 't, yarely, or we run ourselves aground: bestir, bestir.　　　　　*[Exit.*

Enter Mariners.

Boats. Heigh, my hearts! cheerly, cheerly, my hearts! yare, yare! Take in the topsail. Tend to the master's whistle. Blow, till thou burst thy wind, if room enough!

Enter ALONSO, SEBASTIAN, ANTONIO, FERDINAND, GONZALO, *and others.*

Alon. Good boatswain, have care. Where 's the master? Play the men.

Boats. I pray now, keep below.　　　　　　　　　10

Ant. Where is the master, boatswain?

Boats. Do you not hear him? You mar our labour: keep your cabins: you do assist the storm.

Gon. Nay, good, be patient.

Boats. When the sea is. Hence! What cares these

roarers for the name of king? To cabin: silence! trouble
us not.

Gon. Good, yet remember whom thou hast aboard.   18

Boats. None that I more love than myself. You are a
counsellor; if you can command these elements to silence,
and work the peace of the present, we will not hand a rope
more; use your authority: if you cannot, give thanks you
have lived so long, and make yourself ready in your cabin
for the mischance of the hour, if it so hap. Cheerly, good
hearts! Out of our way, I say.   [*Exit.* 25

Gon. I have great comfort from this fellow: methinks he
hath no drowning mark upon him; his complexion is perfect
gallows. Stand fast, good Fate, to his hanging: make the
rope of his destiny our cable, for our own doth little advantage. If he be not born to be hanged, our case is miserable.
          [*Exeunt.*

Re-enter Boatswain.

Boats. Down with the topmast! yare! lower, lower! Bring
her to try with main-course. [*A cry within.*] A plague
upon this howling! they are louder than the weather or our
office.   34

Re-enter SEBASTIAN, ANTONIO, *and* GONZALO.

Yet again! what do you here? Shall we give o'er and
drown? Have you a mind to sink?

Seb. A pox o' your throat, you bawling, blasphemous,
incharitable dog!

Boats. Work you then.

Ant. Hang, cur! hang, you insolent noisemaker!   40
We are less afraid to be drowned than thou art.

Gon. I'll warrant him for drowning; though the ship
were no stronger than a nutshell.

Boats. Lay her a-hold, a-hold! set her two courses off to
sea again; lay her off.

Enter Mariners *wet.*

Mariners. All lost! to prayers, to prayers! all lost!

Boats. What, must our mouths be cold?

Gon. The king and prince at prayers! let's assist them,
For our case is as theirs.

Seb.   I'm out of patience.

Ant. We are merely cheated of our lives by drunkards: 50
This wide-chapp'd rascal—would thou mightst lie drowning
The washing of ten tides!

Gon.   He'll be hang'd yet,
Though every drop of water swear against it
And gape at widest to glut him.

                    [*A confused noise within:* 'Mercy on us!'—
        'We split, we split!'—'Farewell my wife and
            children!'—
        'Farewell, brother!'—'We split, we split, we split!']

Ant. Let's all sink with the king.   57

Seb. Let's take leave of him.   [*Exeunt Ant. and Seb.*

Gon. Now would I give a thousand furlongs of sea for an
acre of barren ground, long heath, brown furze, any thing.
The wills above be done! but I would fain die a dry death.

                                    [*Exeunt.*

SCENE II.   *The island.   Before* PROSPERO'S *cell.*

Enter PROSPERO *and* MIRANDA.

Mir. If by your art, my dearest father, you have
Put the wild waters in this roar, allay them.
The sky, it seems, would pour down stinking pitch,
But that the sea, mounting to the welkin's cheek,
Dashes the fire out. O, I have suffer'd
With those that I saw suffer: a brave vessel,
Who had, no doubt, some noble creature in her,
Dash'd all to pieces. O, the cry did knock

Against my very heart.   Poor souls, they perish'd.
Had I been any god of power, I would   10
Have sunk the sea within the earth or ere
It should the good ship so have swallow'd and
The fraughting souls within her.
 Pros.   Be collected:
No more amazement: tell your piteous heart
There 's no harm done.
 Mir.   O, woe the day!
 Pros.   No harm.
I have done nothing but in care of thee,
Of thee, my dear one, thee, my daughter, who
Art ignorant of what thou art, nought knowing
Of whence I am, nor that I am more better
Than Prospero, master of a full poor cell,   20
And thy no greater father.
 Mir.   More to know
Did never meddle with my thoughts.
 Pros.   'T is time
I should inform thee farther.   Lend thy hand,
And pluck my magic garment from me.   So:
       [*Lays down his mantle.*
Lie there, my art.   Wipe thou thine eyes; have comfort.
The direful spectacle of the wreck, which touch'd
The very virtue of compassion in thee,
I have with such provision in mine art
So safely ordered that there is no soul—
No, not so much perdition as an hair   30
Betid to any creature in the vessel
Which thou heard'st cry, which thou saw'st sink.   Sit down;
For thou must now know farther.
 Mir.   You have often
Begun to tell me what I am, but stopp'd
And left me to a bootless inquisition,
Concluding 'Stay: not yet'.

   Pros.   The hour 's now come;
The very minute bids thee ope thine ear;
Obey and be attentive.   Canst thou remember
A time before we came unto this cell?
I do not think thou canst, for then thou wast not   40
Out three years old.
   Mir.   Certainly, sir, I can.
   Pros. By what? by any other house or person?
Of any thing the image tell me that
Hath kept with thy remembrance.
   Mir.   'T is far off
And rather like a dream than an assurance
That my remembrance warrants.   Had I not
Four or five women once that tended me?
   Pros. Thou hadst, and more, Miranda.   But how is it
That this lives in thy mind?   What seest thou else
In the dark backward and abysm of time?   50
If thou remember'st aught ere thou camest here,
How thou camest here thou mayst.
   Mir.   But that I do not.
   Pros. Twelve year since, Miranda, twelve year since,
Thy father was the Duke of Milan and
A prince of power.
   Mir.   Sir, are not you my father?
   Pros. Thy mother was a piece of virtue, and
She said thou wast my daughter; and thy father
Was Duke of Milan; and thou his only heir
And princess no worse issued.
   Mir.   O the heavens!
What foul play had we, that we came from thence?   60
Or blessed was 't we did?
   Pros.   Both, both, my girl:
By foul play, as thou say'st, were we heaved thence,
But blessedly holp hither.
   Mir.   O, my heart bleeds

To think o' the teen that I have turn'd you to,
Which is from my remembrance!   Please you, farther.

   Pros. My brother and thy uncle, call'd Antonio—
I pray thee, mark me—that a brother should
Be so perfidious!—he whom next thyself
Of all the world I loved and to him put
The manage of my state; as at that time   70
Through all the signories it was the first
And Prospero the prime duke, being so reputed
In dignity, and for the liberal arts
Without a parallel; those being all my study,
The government I cast upon my brother
And to my state grew stranger, being transported
And rapt in secret studies.   Thy false uncle—
Dost thou attend me?
   Mir.   Sir, most heedfully.
   Pros. Being once perfected how to grant suits,
How to deny them, who to advance and who   80
To trash for over-topping, new created
The creatures that were mine, I say, or changed 'em,
Or else new form'd 'em; having both the key
Of officer and office, set all hearts i' the state
To what tune pleased his ear; that now he was
The ivy which had hid my princely trunk,
And suck'd my verdure out on 't.   Thou attend'st not.
   Mir. O, good sir, I do.
   Pros.   I pray thee, mark me.
I, thus neglecting worldly ends, all dedicated
To closeness and the bettering of my mind   90
With that which, but by being so retired,
O'er-prized all popular rate, in my false brother
Awaked an evil nature; and my trust,
Like a good parent, did beget of him
A falsehood in its contrary as great
As my trust was; which had indeed no limit,

A confidence sans bound.   He being thus lorded,
Not only with what my revenue yielded,
But what my power might else exact, like one
Who having into truth, by telling of it,   100
Made such a sinner of his memory,
To credit his own lie, he did believe
He was indeed the duke; out o' the substitution,
And executing the outward face of royalty,
With all prerogative: hence his ambition growing—
Dost thou hear?
     Mir.   Your tale, sir, would cure deafness.
     Pros. To have no screen between this part he play'd
And him he play'd it for, he needs will be
Absolute Milan.   Me, poor man, my library
Was dukedom large enough: of temporal royalties   110
He thinks me now incapable; confederates—
So dry he was for sway—wi' the King of Naples
To give him annual tribute, do him homage,
Subject his coronet to his crown, and bend
The dukedom yet unbow'd—alas, poor Milan!—
To most ignoble stooping.
     Mir.   O the heavens!
     Pros. Mark his condition and the event; then tell me
If this might be a brother.
     Mir.   I should sin
To think but nobly of my grandmother:
Good wombs have borne bad sons.
     Pros.   Now the condition.   120
This King of Naples, being an enemy
To me inveterate, hearkens my brother's suit;
Which was, that he, in lieu o' the premises
Of homage and I know not how much tribute,
Should presently extirpate me and mine
Out of the dukedom and confer fair Milan
With all the honours on my brother: whereon,

A treacherous army levied, one midnight
Fated to the purpose did Antonio open
The gates of Milan, and, i' the dead of darkness,   130
The ministers for the purpose hurried thence
Me and thy crying self.

    Mir.   Alack, for pity!
I, not remembering how I cried out then,
Will cry it o'er again: it is a hint
That wrings mine eyes to 't.

    Pros.   Hear a little further
And then I 'll bring thee to the present business
Which now 's upon 's; without the which this story
Were most impertinent.

    Mir.   Wherefore did they not
That hour destroy us?

    Pros.   Well demanded, wench:
My tale provokes that question. Dear, they durst not,   140
So dear the love my people bore me, nor set
A mark so bloody on the business, but
With colours fairer painted their foul ends.
In few, they hurried us aboard a bark,
Bore us some leagues to sea; where they prepared
A rotten carcass of a butt, not rigg'd,
Nor tackle, sail, nor mast; the very rats
Instinctively have quit it: there they hoist us,
To cry to the sea that roar'd to us, to sigh
To the winds whose pity, sighing back again,   150
Did us but loving wrong.

    Mir.   Alack, what trouble
Was I then to you!

    Pros.   O, a cherubin
Thou wast that did preserve me. Thou didst smile,
Infused with a fortitude from heaven,
When I have deck'd the sea with drops full salt,
Under my burthen groan'd; which raised in me

An undergoing stomach, to bear up
Against what should ensue.
 Mir.   How came we ashore?
 Pros. By Providence divine.
Some food we had and some fresh water that   160
A noble Neapolitan, Gonzalo,
Out of his charity, who being then appointed
Master of this design, did give us, with
Rich garments, linens, stuffs and necessaries,
Which since have steaded much; so, of his gentleness,
Knowing I loved my books, he furnish'd me
From mine own library with volumes that
I prize above my dukedom.
 Mir.   Would I might
But ever see that man!
 Pros.   Now I arise: [*Resumes his mantle.*
Sit still, and hear the last of our sea-sorrow.   170
Here in this island we arrived; and here
Have I, thy schoolmaster, made thee more profit
Than other princesses can that have more time
For vainer hours and tutors not so careful.
 Mir. Heavens thank you for 't! And now, I pray you, sir,
For still 't is beating in my mind, your reason
For raising this sea-storm?
 Pros.   Know thus far forth.
By accident most strange, bountiful Fortune,
Now my dear lady, hath mine enemies
Brought to this shore; and by my prescience   180
I find my zenith doth depend upon
A most auspicious star, whose influence
If now I court not but omit, my fortunes
Will ever after droop. Here cease more questions:
Thou art inclined to sleep: 't is a good dulness,
And give it way: I know thou canst not choose.
            [*Miranda sleeps.*

Come away, servant, come.   I am ready now.
Approach, my Ariel, come.

Enter ARIEL.

Ari. All hail, great master! grave sir, hail! I come
To answer thy best pleasure; be 't to fly,   190
To swim, to dive into the fire, to ride
On the curl'd clouds, to thy strong bidding task
Ariel and all his quality.
    Pros.   Hast thou, spirit,
Perform'd to point the tempest that I bade thee?
    Ari. To every article.
I boarded the king's ship; now on the beak,
Now in the waist, the deck, in every cabin,
I flamed amazement: sometime I 'ld divide,
And burn in many places; on the topmast,
The yards and bowsprit, would I flame distinctly,   200
Then meet and join.   Jove's lightnings, the precursors
O' the dreadful thunder-claps, more momentary
And sight-outrunning were not; the fire and cracks
Of sulphurous roaring the most mighty Neptune
Seem to besiege and make his bold waves tremble,
Yea, his dread trident shake.
    Pros.   My brave spirit!
Who was so firm, so constant, that this coil
Would not infect his reason?
    Ari.   Not a soul
But felt a fever of the mad and play'd
Some tricks of desperation.   All but mariners   210
Plunged in the foaming brine and quit the vessel,
Then all afire with me: the king's son, Ferdinand,
With hair up-staring,—then like reeds, not hair,—
Was the first man that leap'd; cried, 'Hell is empty,
And all the devils are here'.

Pros. Why, that's my spirit!
But was not this nigh shore?
Ari. Close by, my master.
Pros. But are they, Ariel, safe?
Ari. Not a hair perish'd;
On their sustaining garments not a blemish,
But fresher than before: and, as thou badest me,
In troops I have dispersed them 'bout the isle. 220
The king's son have I landed by himself;
Whom I left cooling of the air with sighs
In an odd angle of the isle, and sitting,
His arms in this sad knot.
Pros. Of the king's ship,
The mariners, say how thou hast disposed
And all the rest o' the fleet.
Ari. Safely in harbour
Is the king's ship; in the deep nook, where once
Thou call'dst me up at midnight to fetch dew
From the still-vex'd Bermoothes, there she's hid:
The mariners all under hatches stow'd; 230
Who, with a charm join'd to their suffer'd labour,
I have left asleep: and for the rest o' the fleet
Which I dispersed, they all have met again
And are upon the Mediterranean flote,
Bound sadly home for Naples,
Supposing that they saw the king's ship wreck'd
And his great person perish.
Pros. Ariel, thy charge
Exactly is perform'd: but there's more work.
What is the time o' the day?
Ari. Past the mid season.
Pros. At least two glasses. The time 'twixt six and now
Must by us both be spent most preciously. 241
Ari. Is there more toil? Since thou dost give me
pains,

Let me remember thee what thou hast promised,
Which is not yet perform'd me.

    Pros.   How now? moody?
What is 't thou canst demand?

    Ari.   My liberty.

    Pros. Before the time be out? no more!

    Ari.   I prithee,
Remember I have done thee worthy service;
Told thee no lies, made thee no mistakings, served
Without or grudge or grumblings; thou didst promise
To bate me a full year.

    Pros.   Dost thou forget   250
From what a torment I did free thee?

    Ari.   No.

    Pros. Thou dost, and think'st it much to tread the ooze
Of the salt deep,
To run upon the sharp wind of the north,
To do me business in the veins o' the earth
When it is baked with frost.

    Ari.   I do not, sir.

    Pros. Thou liest, malignant thing! Hast thou forgot
The foul witch Sycorax, who with age and envy
Was grown into a hoop? hast thou forgot her?

    Ari. No, sir.

    Pros.   Thou hast. Where was she born? speak.
    tell me.   260

    Ari. Sir, in Argier.

    Pros.   O, was she so? I must
Once in a month recount what thou hast been,
Which thou forget'st. This damn'd witch Sycorax,
For mischiefs manifold and sorceries terrible
To enter human hearing, from Argier,
Thou know'st, was banish'd: for one thing she did
They would not take her life. Is not this true?

    Ari. Ay, sir.

Pros. This blue-eyed hag was hither brought with child
And here was left by the sailors.   Thou, my slave,   270
As thou report'st thyself, wast then her servant;
And, for thou wast a spirit too delicate
To act her earthy and abhorr'd commands,
Refusing her grand hests, she did confine thee,
By help of her more potent ministers
And in her most unmitigable rage,
Into a cloven pine; within which rift
Imprison'd thou didst painfully remain
A dozen years; within which space she died
And left thee there; where thou didst vent thy groans   280
As fast as mill-wheels strike.   Then was this island—
Save for the son that she did litter here,
A freckled whelp hag-born—not honour'd with
A human shape.
       Ari.   Yes, Caliban her son.
   Pros. Dull thing, I say so; he, that Caliban
Whom now I keep in service.   Thou best know'st
What torment I did find thee in; thy groans
Did make wolves howl and penetrate the breasts
Of ever angry bears: it was a torment
To lay upon the damn'd, which Sycorax   290
Could not again undo: it was mine art,
When I arrived and heard thee, that made gape
The pine and let thee out.
       Ari.   I thank thee, master.
   Pros. If thou more murmur'st, I will rend an oak
And peg thee in his knotty entrails till
Thou hast howl'd away twelve winters.
       Ari.   Pardon, master,
I will be correspondent to command
And do my spiriting gently.
       Pros.   Do so, and after two days
I will discharge thee.

Ari.   That's my noble master!
What shall I do! say what; what shall I do?   300
    Pros. Go make thyself like a nymph o' the sea: be subject
To no sight but thine and mine, invisible
To every eyeball else.   Go take this shape
And hither come in 't: go, hence with diligence!
                                              [*Exit Ariel.*
Awake, dear heart, awake! thou hast slept well;
Awake!
    Mir.   The strangeness of your story put
Heaviness in me.
    Pros.   Shake it off.   Come on;
We 'll visit Caliban my slave, who never
Yields us kind answer.
    Mir.   'T is a villain, sir,
I do not love to look on.
    Pros.   But, as 't is,   310
We cannot miss him: he does make our fire,
Fetch in our wood and serves in offices
That profit us.   What ho! slave! Caliban!
Thou earth, thou! speak.
    Cal.   [*Within*] There 's wood enough within.
    Pros. Come forth, I say! there 's other business for thee:
Come, thou tortoise! when?

                Re-enter ARIEL *like a water-nymph.*

Fine apparition!   My quaint Ariel,
Hark in thine ear.
    Ari.   My lord, it shall be done.   [*Exit.*
    Pros. Thou poisonous slave, got by the devil himself
Upon thy wicked dam, come forth!   320

                Enter CALIBAN.

    Cal. As wicked dew as e'er my mother brush'd
With raven's feather from unwholesome fen

Drop on you both! a south-west blow on ye
And blister you all o'er!

 Pros. For this, be sure, to-night thou shalt have cramps,
Side-stitches that shall pen thy breath up; urchins
Shall, for that vast of night that they may work,
All exercise on thee; thou shalt be pinch'd
As thick as honeycomb, each pinch more stinging
Than bees that made 'em.

 Cal.   I must eat my dinner. 330
This island's mine, by Sycorax my mother,
Which thou takest from me.   When thou camest first,
Thou strok'dst me and mad'st much of me, wouldst give
  me
Water with berries in't, and teach me how
To name the bigger light, and how the less,
That burn by day and night: and then I loved thee
And show'd thee all the qualities o' the isle,
The fresh springs, brine-pits, barren place and fertile:
Cursed be I that did so!   All the charms
Of Sycorax, toads, beetles, bats, light on you! 340
For I am all the subjects that you have,
Which first was mine own king: and here you sty me
In this hard rock, whiles you do keep from me
The rest o' the island.

 Pros.   Thou most lying slave,
Whom stripes may move, not kindness! I have used thee,
Filth as thou art, with human care, and lodged thee
In mine own cell, till thou didst seek to violate
The honour of my child.

 Cal. O ho, O ho! would 't had been done!
Thou didst prevent me; I had peopled else 350
This isle with Calibans.

 Pros.   Abhorred slave,
Which any print of goodness wilt not take,
Being capable of all ill!   I pitied thee,

Took pains to make thee speak, taught thee each hour
One thing or other: when thou didst not, savage,
Know thine own meaning, but wouldst gabble like
A thing most brutish, I endow'd thy purposes
With words that made them known.   But thy vile race,
Though thou didst learn, had that in 't which good natures
Could not abide to be with; therefore wast thou   360
Deservedly confined into this rock,
Who hadst deserved more than a prison.

    Cal. You taught me language; and my profit on 't
Is, I know how to curse.   The red plague rid you
For learning me your language!

    Pros.   Hag-seed, hence!
Fetch us in fuel; and be quick, thou 'rt best,
To answer other business.   Shrug'st thou, malice?
If thou neglect'st or dost unwillingly
What I command, I 'll rack thee with old cramps,
Fill all thy bones with aches, make thee roar   370
That beasts shall tremble at thy din.

    Cal.   No, pray thee.
[*Aside*] I must obey: his art is of such power,
It would control my dam's god, Setebos,
And make a vassal of him.

    Pros.   So, slave; hence! [*Exit Caliban.*

Re-enter ARIEL, *invisible, playing and singing;* FERDINAND
following.

ARIEL'S *song.*

> Come unto these yellow sands,
>   And then take hands:
> Courtsied when you have and kiss'd
>   The wild waves whist,
> Foot it featly here and there;
> And, sweet sprites, the burthen bear.   380

Burthen [*dispersedly*]. Hark, hark!

Bow-wow.

    The watch-dogs bark:

Bow-wow.

  Ari. Hark, hark! I hear
      The strain of strutting chanticleer
      Cry, Cock-a-diddle-dow.

  Fer. Where should this music be? i' the air or the earth?
It sounds no more: and, sure, it waits upon
Some god o' the island.   Sitting on a bank,
Weeping again the king my father's wreck,
This music crept by me upon the waters,   390
Allaying both their fury and my passion
With its sweet air: thence I have follow'd it,
Or it hath drawn me rather.   But 't is gone.
No, it begins again.

ARIEL sings.

    Full fathom five thy father lies;
      Of his bones are coral made;
    Those are pearls that were his eyes:
      Nothing of him that doth fade
    But doth suffer a sea-change
    Into something rich and strange.   400
    Sea-nymphs hourly ring his knell:

Burthen. Ding-dong.

  Ari. Hark! now I hear them,—Ding-dong, bell.

  Fer. The ditty does remember my drown'd father.
This is no mortal business, nor no sound
That the earth owes.   I hear it now above me.

  Pros. The fringéd curtains of thine eye advance
And say what thou seest yond.

  Mir.   What is 't? a spirit?
Lord, how it looks about!   Believe me, sir,
It carries a brave form.   But 't is a spirit.   410

Pros. No, wench; it eats and sleeps and hath such senses
As we have, such.   This gallant which thou seest
Was in the wreck; and, but he 's something stain'd
With grief that 's beauty's canker, thou mightst call him
A goodly person: he hath lost his fellows
And strays about to find 'em.
    Mir.   I might call him
A thing divine, for nothing natural
I ever saw so noble.
    Pros.   [*Aside*] It goes on, I see,
As my soul prompts it.   Spirit, fine spirit! I 'll free thee
Within two days for this.
    Fer.   Most sure, the goddess   420
On whom these airs attend!   Vouchsafe my prayer
May know if you remain upon this island;
And that you will some good instruction give
How I may bear me here: my prime request,
Which I do last pronounce, is, O you wonder!
If you be maid or no?
    Mir.   No wonder, sir;
But certainly a maid.
    Fer.   My language! heavens!
I am the best of them that speak this speech,
Were I but where 't is spoken.
    Pros.   How? the best?
What wert thou, if the King of Naples heard thee?   430
    Fer. A single thing, as I am now, that wonders
To hear thee speak of Naples.   He does hear me;
And that he does I weep: myself am Naples,
Who with mine eyes, never since at ebb, beheld
The king my father wreck'd.
    Mir.   Alack, for mercy!
    Fer. Yes, faith, and all his lords; the Duke of Milan
And his brave son being twain.
    Pros   [*Aside*] The Duke of Milan

And his more braver daughter could control thee,
If now 't were fit to do 't.   At the first sight
They have changed eyes.   Delicate Ariel,   440
I 'll set thee free for this.   [*To Fer.*] A word, good sir;
I fear you have done yourself some wrong: a word.

    Mir. Why speaks my father so ungently?   This
Is the third man that e'er I saw, the first
That e'er I sighed for: pity move my father
To be inclined my way!

    Fer.   O, if a virgin,
And your affection not gone forth, I 'll make you
The queen of Naples.

    Pros.   Soft, sir! one word more.
[*Aside*] They are both in either's powers; but this swift business
I must uneasy make, lest too light winning   450
Make the prize light.   [*To Fer.*] One word more: I charge
    thee
That thou attend me: thou dost here usurp
The name thou owest not; and hast put thyself
Upon this island as a spy, to win it
From me, the lord on 't.

    Fer.   No, as I am a man.

    Mir. There 's nothing ill can dwell in such a temple:
If the ill spirit have so fair a house,
Good things will strive to dwell with 't.

    Pros.   Follow me.
Speak not you for him; he 's a traitor.   Come;
I 'll manacle thy neck and feet together: 460
Sea-water shalt thou drink; thy food shall be
The fresh-brook mussels, wither'd roots and husks
Wherein the acorn cradled.   Follow.

    Fer.   No;
I will resist such entertainment till
Mine enemy has more power.

               [*Draws, and is charmed from moving.*

Mir.   O dear father.
Make not too rash a trial of him, for
He's gentle and not fearful.
      Pros.   What? I say,
My foot my tutor! Put thy sword up, traitor;
Who makest a show but darest not strike, thy conscience
Is so possess'd with guilt: come from thy ward,   470
For I can here disarm thee with this stick
And make thy weapon drop.
      Mir.   Beseech you, father.
      Pros. Hence! hang not on my garments.
      Mir.   Sir, have pity;
I'll be his surety.
      Pros.   Silence! one word more
Shall make me chide thee, if not hate thee. What!
An advocate for an impostor! hush!
Thou think'st there is no more such shapes as he,
Having seen but him and Caliban: foolish wench!
To the most of men this is a Caliban
And they to him are angels.
      Mir.   My affections   480
Are then most humble; I have no ambition
To see a goodlier man.
      Pros.   Come on; obey:
Thy nerves are in their infancy again
And have no vigour in them.
      Fer.   So they are;
My spirits, as in a dream, are all bound up.
My father's loss, the weakness which I feel,
The wreck of all my friends, nor this man's threats,
To whom I am subdued, are but light to me,
Might I but through my prison once a day
Behold this maid: all corners else o' the earth   490
Let liberty make use of; space enough
Have I in such a prison.

Pros.   [*Aside*] It works.   [*To Fer.*] Come on.
Thou hast done well, fine Ariel!   [*To Fer.*] Follow me.
[*To Ari.*] Hark what thou else shalt do me.
  Mir.   Be of comfort;
My father's of a better nature, sir,
Than he appears by speech: this is unwonted
Which now came from him.
  Pros.   Thou shalt be as free
As mountain winds: but then exactly do
All points of my command.
  Ari.   To the syllable.
  Pros. Come, follow.   Speak not for him.   [*Exeunt.* 500

ACT II.

SCENE I.   *Another part of the island.*

Enter ALONSO, SEBASTIAN, ANTONIO, GONZALO, ADRIAN,
FRANCISCO, *and others.*

  Gon. Beseech you, sir, be merry; you have cause,
So have we all, of joy; for our escape
Is much beyond our loss.   Our hint of woe
Is common; every day some sailor's wife,
The masters of some merchant and the merchant
Have just our theme of woe; but for the miracle,
I mean our preservation, few in millions
Can speak like us: then wisely, good sir, weigh
Our sorrow with our comfort.
  Alon.   Prithee, peace.
  Seb. He receives comfort like cold porridge.   10
  Ant. The visitor will not give him o'er so.
  Seb. Look, he's winding up the watch of his wit; by and
by it will strike.

Gon. Sir,—

Seb. One; tell.

Gon. When every grief is entertain'd that 's offer'd,
Comes to the entertainer—

Seb. A dollar.

Gon. Dolour comes to him, indeed; you have spoken
truer than you purposed.   20

Seb. You have taken it wiselier than I meant you should.

Gon. Therefore, my lord,—

Ant. Fie, what a spendthrift is he of his tongue!

Alon. I prithee, spare.

Gon. Well, I have done: but yet,—

Seb. He will be talking.

Ant. Which, of he or Adrian, for a good wager, first
begins to crow?

Seb. The old cock.

Ant. The cockerel.   30

Seb. Done. The wager?

Ant. A laughter.

Seb. A match!

Adr. Though this island seem to be desert,—

Seb. Ha, ha, ha! So, you 're paid.

Adr. Uninhabitable and almost inaccessible,—

Seb. Yet,—

Adr. Yet,—

Ant. He could not miss 't.

Adr. It must needs be of subtle, tender and delicate
temperance.   41

Ant. Temperance was a delicate wench.

Seb. Ay, and a subtle; as he most learnedly delivered.

Adr. The air breathes upon us here most sweetly.

Seb. As if it had lungs and rotten ones.

Ant. Or as 't were perfumed by a fen.

Gon. Here is everything advantageous to life.

Ant. True; save means to live.

Seb. Of that there's none, or little.

Gon. How lush and lusty the grass looks! how green! 50

Ant. The ground indeed is tawny.

Seb. With an eye of green in 't.

Ant. He misses not much.

Seb. No; he doth but mistake the truth totally.

Gon. But the rarity of it is, — which is indeed almost beyond credit,—

Seb. As many vouched rarities are.

Gon. That our garments, being, as they were, drenched in the sea, hold notwithstanding their freshness and glosses, being rather new-dyed than stained with salt water. 60

Ant. If but one of his pockets could speak, would it not say he lies?

Seb. Ay, or very falsely pocket up his report.

Gon. Methinks our garments are now as fresh as when we put them on first in Afric, at the marriage of the king's fair daughter Claribel to the King of Tunis.

Seb. 'T was a sweet marriage, and we prosper well in our return.

Adr. Tunis was never graced before with such a paragon to their queen. 70

Gon. Not since widow Dido's time.

Ant. Widow! a pox o' that! How came that widow in? widow Dido!

Seb. What if he had said 'widower Æneas' too? Good Lord, how you take it!

Adr. 'Widow Dido' said you? you make me study of that; she was of Carthage, not of Tunis.

Gon. This Tunis, sir, was Carthage.

Adr. Carthage?

Gon. I assure you, Carthage. 80

Seb. His word is more than the miraculous harp; he hath raised the wall and houses too.

Ant. What impossible matter will he make easy next?

Seb. I think he will carry this island home in his pocket and give it his son for an apple.

Ant. And, sowing the kernels of it in the sea, bring forth more islands.

Alon. Ay.

Ant. Why, in good time.

Gon. Sir, we were talking that our garments seem now as fresh as when we were at Tunis at the marriage of your daughter, who is now queen.   92

Ant. And the rarest that e'er came there.

Seb. Bate, I beseech you, widow Dido.

Ant. O, widow Dido! ay, widow Dido.

Gon. Is not, sir, my doublet as fresh as the first day I wore it?   I mean, in a sort.

Ant. That sort was well fished for.

Gon. When I wore it at your daughter's marriage?

Alon. You cram these words into mine ears against   100
The stomach of my sense.   Would I had never
Married my daughter there! for, coming thence,
My son is lost and, in my rate, she too,
Who is so far from Italy removed
I ne'er again shall see her.   O thou mine heir
Of Naples and of Milan, what strange fish
Hath made his meal on thee?

   Fran.   Sir, he may live:
I saw him beat the surges under him,
And ride upon their backs; he trod the water,
Whose enmity he flung aside, and breasted   110
The surge most swollen that met him; his bold head
'Bove the contentious waves he kept, and oar'd
Himself with his good arms in lusty stroke
To the shore, that o'er his wave-worn basis bow'd,
As stooping to relieve him: I not doubt
He came alive to land.

   Alon.   No, no, he's gone.

Seb. Sir, you may thank yourself for this great loss,
That would not bless our Europe with your daughter,
But rather lose her to an African;
Where she at least is banish'd from your eye,   120
Who hath cause to wet the grief on 't.
          Alon.   Prithee, peace.
     Seb. You were kneel'd to and importuned otherwise
By all of us, and the fair soul herself
Weigh'd between loathness and obedience, at
Which end o' the beam should bow. We have lost your son,
I fear, for ever: Milan and Naples have
Moe widows in them of this business' making
Than we bring men to comfort them:
The fault 's your own.
          Alon.   So is the dear'st o' the loss.
     Gon. My lord Sebastian,   130
The truth you speak doth lack some gentleness
And time to speak it in: you rub the sore,
When you should bring the plaster.
          Seb.   Very well.
     Ant. And most chirurgeonly.
     Gon. It is foul weather in us all, good sir,
When you are cloudy.
          Seb.   Foul weather?
          Ant.   Very foul.
     Gon. Had I plantation of this isle, my lord,—
     Ant. He 'ld sow 't with nettle-seed.
          Seb.   Or docks, or mallows.
     Gon. And were the king on 't, what would I do?
     Seb. 'Scape being drunk for want of wine.   140
     Gon. I' the commonwealth I would by contraries
Execute all things; for no kind of traffic
Would I admit; no name of magistrate:
Letters should not be known; riches, poverty,
And use of service, none: contract, succession,

Bourn, bound of land, tilth, vineyard, none;
No use of metal, corn, or wine, or oil;
No occupation: all men idle, all;
And women too, but innocent and pure;
No sovereignty;—

Seb.   Yet he would be king on 't.   150

Ant. The latter end of his commonwealth forgets the beginning.

Gon. All things in common nature should produce
Without sweat or endeavour: treason, felony,
Sword, pike, knife, gun, or need of any engine,
Would I not have; but nature should bring forth,
Of it own kind, all foison, all abundance,
To feed my innocent people.

Seb. No marrying 'mong his subjects?

Ant. None, man; all idle.   160

Gon. I would with such perfection govern, sir,
To excel the golden age.

Seb.   Save his majesty!

Ant. Long live Gonzalo.

Gon.   And,—do you mark me, sir?

Alon. Prithee, no more: thou dost talk nothing to me.

Gon. I do well believe your highness; and did it to minister occasion to these gentlemen, who are of such sensible and nimble lungs that they always use to laugh at nothing.

Ant. 'T was you we laughed at.

Gon. Who in this kind of merry fooling am nothing to you: so you may continue and laugh at nothing still.   170

Ant. What a blow was there given!

Seb. An it had not fallen flat-long.

Gon. You are gentlemen of brave mettle; you would lift the moon out of her sphere, if she would continue in it five weeks without changing.

Enter ARIEL, *invisible, playing solemn music.*

Seb. We would so, and then go a bat-fowling.

Ant. Nay, good my lord, be not angry.

Gon. No, I warrant you; I will not adventure my discretion
so weakly. Will you laugh me asleep, for I am very heavy?

Ant. Go sleep, and hear us.   180

              [*All sleep except Alon., Seb., and Ant.*

Alon. What, all so soon asleep! I wish mine eyes
Would, with themselves, shut up my thoughts: I find
They are inclined to do so.

Seb.   Please you, sir,
Do not omit the heavy offer of it:
It seldom visits sorrow; when it doth,
It is a comforter.

Ant.   We two, my lord,
Will guard your person while you take your rest,
And watch your safety.

Alon.   Thank you. Wondrous heavy.

              [*Alonso sleeps.   Exit Ariel.*

Seb. What a strange drowsiness possesses them!

Ant. It is the quality o' the climate.

Seb.   Why   190
Doth it not then our eyelids sink? I find not
Myself disposed to sleep.

Ant.   Nor I; my spirits are nimble.
They fell together all, as by consent;
They dropp'd, as by a thunder-stroke. What might,
Worthy Sebastian? O, what might?—No more:—
And yet methinks I see it in thy face,
What thou shouldst be: the occasion speaks thee, and
My strong imagination sees a crown
Dropping upon thy head.

Seb.   What, art thou waking?

Ant. Do you not hear me speak?

Seb.   I do; and surely   200
It is a sleepy language and thou speak'st
Out of thy sleep. What is it thou didst say?
This is a strange repose, to be asleep
With eyes wide open; standing, speaking, moving,
And yet so fast asleep.

Ant.   Noble Sebastian,
Thou let'st thy fortune sleep—die, rather; wink'st
Whiles thou art waking.

Seb.   Thou dost snore distinctly;
There's meaning in thy snores.

Ant. I am more serious than my custom: you
Must be so too, if heed me; which to do   210
Trebles thee o'er.

Seb.   Well, I am standing water.

Ant. I'll teach you how to flow.

Seb.   Do so: to ebb
Hereditary sloth instructs me.

Ant.   O,
If you but knew how you the purpose cherish
Whiles thus you mock it! how, in stripping it,
You more invest it! Ebbing men, indeed,
Most often do so near the bottom run
By their own fear or sloth.

Seb.   Prithee, say on:
The setting of thine eye and cheek proclaim
A matter from thee, and a birth indeed   220
Which throes thee much to yield.

Ant.   Thus, sir:
Although this lord of weak remembrance, this,
Who shall be of as little memory
When he is earth'd, hath here almost persuaded,—
For he's a spirit of persuasion, only
Professes to persuade,—the king his son's alive,

'T is as impossible that he 's undrown'd
As he that sleeps here swims.
　　Seb.　　　　　　　　I have no hope
That he 's undrown'd.
　　Ant.　　　　　　　O, out of that 'no hope'
What great hope have you! no hope that way is　　230
Another way so high a hope that even
Ambition cannot pierce a wink beyond,
But doubt discovery there.　Will you grant with me
That Ferdinand is drown'd?
　　Seb.　　　　　　　　He 's gone.
　　Ant.　　　　　　　　　Then, tell me,
Who 's the next heir of Naples?
　　Seb.　　　　　　　　Claribel.
　　Ant. She that is queen of Tunis; she that dwells
Ten leagues beyond man's life; she that from Naples
Can have no note, unless the sun were post—
The man i' the moon 's too slow—till new-born chins
Be rough and razorable; she that—from whom　　240
We all were sea-swallow'd, though some cast again,
And by that destiny to perform an act
Whereof what 's past is prologue, what to come
In yours and my discharge.
　　Seb.　　　　　　　What stuff is this! how say you?
'T is true, my brother's daughter 's queen of Tunis;
So is she heir of Naples; 'twixt which regions
There is some space.
　　Ant.　　　　　　A space whose every cubit
Seems to cry out, 'How shall that Claribel
Measure us back to Naples?　Keep in Tunis,
And let Sebastian wake.'　Say, this were death　　250
That now hath seized them; why, they were no worse
Than now they are.　There be that can rule Naples
As well as he that sleeps; lords that can prate
As amply and unnecessarily

As this Gonzalo; I myself could make
A chough of as deep chat.   O, that you bore
The mind that I do! what a sleep were this
For your advancement!   Do you understand me?

Seb. Methinks I do.

Ant.   And how does your content
Tender your own good fortune?

Seb.   I remember   260
You did supplant your brother Prospero.

Ant.   True:
And look how well my garments sit upon me;
Much feater than before: my brother's servants
Were then my fellows; now they are my men.

Seb. But, for your conscience?

Ant. Ay, sir; where lies that? if 't were a kibe,
'T would put me to my slipper: but I feel not
This deity in my bosom: twenty consciences,
That stand 'twixt me and Milan, candied be they
And melt ere they molest!   Here lies your brother,   270
No better than the earth he lies upon,
If he were that which now he's like, that's dead;
Whom I, with this obedient steel, three inches of it,
Can lay to bed for ever; whiles you, doing thus,
To the perpetual wink for aye might put
This ancient morsel, this Sir Prudence, who
Should not upbraid our course.   For all the rest,
They'll take suggestion as a cat laps milk;
They'll tell the clock to any business that
We say befits the hour.

Seb.   Thy case, dear friend,   280
Shall be my precedent; as thou got'st Milan,
I'll come by Naples.   Draw thy sword: one stroke
Shall free thee from the tribute which thou payest:
And I the king shall love thee.

Ant.   Draw together;

And when I rear my hand, do you the like,
To fall it on Gonzalo.
　　Seb.　　　　　　O, but one word.　　[*They talk apart.*

　　　　　　Re-enter ARIEL, *invisible.*

　　Ari. My master through his art foresees the danger
That you, his friend, are in; and sends me forth—
For else his project dies—to keep them living.
　　　　　　　　　　　　[*Sings in Gonzalo's ear.*
　　　　　　　While you here do snoring lie,　　　　290
　　　　　　　Open-eyed conspiracy
　　　　　　　　　His time doth take.
　　　　　　　If of life you keep a care,
　　　　　　　Shake off slumber, and beware:
　　　　　　　　Awake, awake!
　　Ant. Then let us both be sudden.
　　Gon.　　　　　　　　　　Now, good angels
Preserve the king.　　　　　　　　　　[*They wake.*
　　Alon. Why, how now? ho, awake! Why are you
　　　drawn?
Wherefore this ghastly looking?
　　Gon.　　　　　　　　What's the matter?
　　Seb. Whiles we stood here securing your repose,　　300
Even now, we heard a hollow burst of bellowing
Like bulls, or rather lions: did't not wake you?
It struck mine ear most terribly.
　　Alon.　　　　　　　I heard nothing.
　　Ant. O, 'twas a din to fright a monster's ear,
To make an earthquake! sure, it was the roar
Of a whole herd of lions.
　　Alon.　　　　　　Heard you this, Gonzalo?
　　Gon. Upon mine honour, sir, I heard a humming,
And that a strange one too, which did awake me:
I shaked you, sir, and cried: as mine eyes open'd,
I saw their weapons drawn: there was a noise,　　310

That's verily. 'T is best we stand upon our guard,
Or that we quit this place: let's draw our weapons.

 Alon. Lead off this ground; and let's make further search
For my poor son.

 Gon.   Heavens keep him from these beasts!
For he is, sure, i' the island.

 Alon.   Lead away.

 Ari. Prospero my lord shall know what I have done:
So, king, go safely on to seek thy son.   *[Exeunt.*

Scene II. *Another part of the island.*

Enter Caliban *with a burden of wood. A noise of thunder
heard.*

 Cal. All the infections that the sun sucks up
From bogs, fens, flats, on Prosper fall and make him
By inch-meal a disease! His spirits hear me
And yet I needs must curse. But they'll nor pinch,
Fright me with urchin-shows, pitch me i' the mire,
Nor lead me, like a firebrand, in the dark
Out of my way, unless he bid 'em; but
For every trifle are they set upon me;
Sometime like apes that mow and chatter at me
And after bite me, then like hedgehogs which   10
Lie tumbling in my barefoot way and mount
Their pricks at my footfall; sometime am I
All wound with adders who with cloven tongues
Do hiss me into madness.

Enter Trinculo.

     Lo, now, lo!
Here comes a spirit of his, and to torment me
For bringing wood in slowly. I'll fall flat;
Perchance he will not mind me.   17

 Trin. Here's neither bush nor shrub, to bear off any

weather at all, and another storm brewing; I hear it sing i'
the wind: yond same black cloud, yond huge one, looks like
a foul bombard that would shed his liquor. If it should
thunder as it did before, I know not where to hide my head:
yond same cloud cannot choose but fall by pailfuls. What
have we here? a man or a fish? dead or alive? A fish:
he smells like a fish; a very ancient and fish-like smell; a
kind of not of the newest Poor-John. A strange fish! Were
I in England now, as once I was, and had but this fish
painted, not a holiday fool there but would give a piece of
silver: there would this monster make a man; any strange
beast there makes a man: when they will not give a doit to
relieve a lame beggar, they will lay out ten to see a dead
Indian. Legged like a man! and his fins like arms! Warm,
o' my troth! I do now let loose my opinion; hold it no
longer: this is no fish, but an islander, that hath lately
suffered by a thunderbolt. [*Thunder.*] Alas, the storm is
come again! my best way is to creep under his gaberdine;
there is no other shelter hereabout: misery acquaints a man
with strange bed-fellows. I will here shroud till the dregs
of the storm be past.   39

Enter STEPHANO, *singing: a bottle in his hand.*

Ste.   I shall no more to sea, to sea,
          Here shall I die ashore—

This is a very scurvy tune to sing at a man's funeral: well,
here 's my comfort.   [*Drinks.*
[*Sings.*

          The master, the swabber, the boatswain and I,
              The gunner and his mate
          Loved Mall, Meg and Marian and Margery,
              But none of us cared for Kate;
              For she had a tongue with a tang,
              Would cry to a sailor, Go hang!

She loved not the savour of tar nor of pitch,   50
    Then to sea, boys, and let her go hang!
This is a scurvy tune too: but here's my comfort. [*Drinks.*

Cal. Do not torment me: Oh!

Ste. What's the matter? Have we devils here? Do you put tricks upon 's with savages and men of Ind, ha? I have not 'scaped drowning to be afeard now of your four legs; for it hath been said, As proper a man as ever went on four legs cannot make him give ground; and it shall be said so again while Stephano breathes at nostrils.

Cal. The spirit torments me; Oh!   60

Ste. This is some monster of the isle with four legs, who hath got, as I take it, an ague. Where the devil should he learn our language? I will give him some relief, if it be but for that. If I can recover him and keep him tame and get to Naples with him, he's a present for any emperor that ever trod on neat's-leather.

Cal. Do not torment me, prithee; I'll bring my wood home faster.   68

Ste. He's in his fit now and does not talk after the wisest. He shall taste of my bottle: if he have never drunk wine afore, it will go near to remove his fit. If I can recover him and keep him tame, I will not take too much for him; he shall pay for him that hath him, and that soundly.

Cal. Thou dost me yet but little hurt; thou wilt anon, I know it by thy trembling: now Prosper works upon thee.

Ste. Come on your ways; open your mouth; here is that which will give language to you, cat: open your mouth; this will shake your shaking, I can tell you, and that soundly: you cannot tell who's your friend: open your chaps again.

Trin. I should know that voice: it should be—but he is drowned; and these are devils: O defend me!   81

Ste. Four legs and two voices: a most delicate monster! His forward voice now is to speak well of his friend; his backward voice is to utter foul speeches and to detract. If

all the wine in my bottle will recover him, I will help his ague.
Come.   Amen!   I will pour some in thy other mouth.

Trin. Stephano!

Ste. Doth thy other mouth call me?   Mercy, mercy!   This
is a devil, and no monster: I will leave him; I have no long
spoon.   90

Trin. Stephano!   If thou beest Stephano, touch me and
speak to me; for I am Trinculo—be not afeard—thy good
friend Trinculo.

Ste. If thou beest Trinculo, come forth: I'll pull thee by
the lesser legs: if any be Trinculo's legs, these are they.
Thou art very Trinculo indeed!   How camest thou?

Trin. I took him to be killed with a thunder-stroke.   But
art thou not drowned, Stephano?   I hope now thou art not
drowned.   Is the storm overblown?   I hid me under the
dead moon-calf's gaberdine for fear of the storm.   And
art thou living, Stephano?   O Stephano, two Neapolitans
scaped!

Ste. Prithee, do not turn me about; my stomach is not
constant.   104

Cal. [*Aside*] These be fine things, an if they be not sprites.
That's a brave god and bears celestial liquor.
I will kneel to him.

Ste. How didst thou 'scape?   How camest thou hither?
swear by this bottle how thou camest hither.   I escaped upon
a butt of sack which the sailors heaved o'erboard, by this
bottle! which I made of the bark of a tree with mine own
hands since I was cast ashore.   112

Cal. I'll swear upon that bottle to be thy true subject;
for the liquor is not earthly.

Ste. Here; swear then how thou escapedst.

Trin. Swum ashore, man, like a duck: I can swim like a
duck, I'll be sworn.

Ste. Here, kiss the book.   Though thou canst swim like
a duck, thou art made like a goose.

Trin. O Stephano, hast any more of this?   120

Ste. The whole butt, man: my cellar is in a rock by the sea-side where my wine is hid.   How now, moon-calf! how does thine ague?

Cal. Hast thou not dropp'd from heaven?

Ste. Out o' the moon, I do assure thee: I was the man i' the moon when time was.

Cal. I have seen thee in her and I do adore thee:
My mistress show'd me thee and thy dog and thy bush.

Ste. Come, swear to that; kiss the book: I will furnish it anon with new contents: swear.   130

Trin. By this good light, this is a very shallow monster! I afeard of him!   A very weak monster!   The man i' the moon!   A most poor credulous monster!   Well drawn, monster, in good sooth!

Cal. I'll show thee every fertile inch o' th' island:
And I will kiss thy foot: I prithee, be my god.

Trin. By this light, a most perfidious and drunken monster! when's god's asleep, he'll rob his bottle.

Cal. I'll kiss thy foot; I'll swear myself thy subject.

Ste. Come on then; down, and swear.   140

Trin. I shall laugh myself to death at this puppy-headed monster.   A most scurvy monster!   I could find in my heart to beat him,—

Ste. Come, kiss.

Trin. But that the poor monster's in drink: an abominable monster!

Cal. I'll show thee the best springs; I'll pluck thee berries;
I'll fish for thee and get thee wood enough.
A plague upon the tyrant that I serve!
I'll bear him no more sticks, but follow thee,   150
Thou wondrous man.

Trin. A most ridiculous monster, to make a wonder of a poor drunkard!

Cal. I prithee, let me bring thee where crabs grow;

And I with my long nails will dig thee pig-nuts;
Show thee a jay's nest and instruct thee how
To snare the nimble marmoset; I 'll bring thee
To clustering filberts and sometimes I 'll get thee
Young scamels from the rock.   Wilt thou go with me? 159
   Ste. I prithee now, lead the way without any more talking.
Trinculo, the king and all our company else being drowned,
we will inherit here: here; bear my bottle: fellow Trinculo,
we 'll fill him by and by again.

   Cal. [*Sings drunkenly*]

      Farewell, master; farewell, farewell!
Trin.   A howling monster; a drunken monster!
Cal.   No more dams I 'll make for fish;
      Nor fetch in firing
      At requiring;
     Nor scrape trencher, nor wash dish:
      'Ban, 'Ban, Cacaliban   170
      Has a new master: get a new man.

Freedom, hey-day! hey-day, freedom! freedom, hey-day,
   freedom!
   Ste. O brave monster!   Lead the way.   [*Exeunt.*

ACT III.

Scene I.   *Before* Prospero's *cell.*

Enter Ferdinand, *bearing a log.*

   Fer. There be some sports are painful, and their labour
Delight in them sets off: some kinds of baseness
Are nobly undergone, and most poor matters
Point to rich ends.   This my mean task
Would be as heavy to me as odious, but

The mistress which I serve quickens what's dead
And makes my labours pleasures: O, she is
Ten times more gentle than her father's crabb'd,
And he's composed of harshness.   I must remove
Some thousands of these logs and pile them up,   10
Upon a sore injunction: my sweet mistress
Weeps when she sees me work, and says, such baseness
Had never like executor.   I forget:
But these sweet thoughts do even refresh my labours,
Most busy lest, when I do it.

> *Enter* MIRANDA; *and* PROSPERO *at a distance, unseen.*

  Mir.   Alas, now, pray you,
Work not so hard: I would the lightning had
Burnt up those logs that you are enjoin'd to pile!
Pray, set it down and rest you: when this burns,
'T will weep for having wearied you.   My father
Is hard at study; pray now, rest yourself;   20
He's safe for these three hours.
  Fer.   O most dear mistress,
The sun will set before I shall discharge
What I must strive to do.
  Mir.   If you'll sit down,
I'll bear your logs the while: pray, give me that;
I'll carry it to the pile.
  Fer.   No, precious creature;
I had rather crack my sinews, break my back,
Than you should such dishonour undergo,
While I sit lazy by.
  Mir.   It would become me
As well as it does you: and I should do it
With much more ease; for my good will is to it,   30
And yours it is against.
  Pros.   Poor worm, thou art infected!
This visitation shows it.

Mir.   You look wearily.

Fer. No, noble mistress; 'tis fresh morning with me
When you are by at night. I do beseech you—
Chiefly that I might set it in my prayers—
What is your name?

Mir.   Miranda.—O my father,
I have broke your hest to say so!

Fer.   Admired Miranda!
Indeed the top of admiration! worth
What's dearest to the world! Full many a lady
I have eyed with best regard, and many a time   40
The harmony of their tongues hath into bondage
Brought my too diligent ear: for several virtues
Have I liked several women; never any
With so full soul, but some defect in her
Did quarrel with the noblest grace she owed
And put it to the foil: but you, O you,
So perfect and so peerless, are created
Of every creature's best!

Mir.   I do not know
One of my sex; no woman's face remember,
Save, from my glass, mine own; nor have I seen   50
More that I may call men than you, good friend,
And my dear father: how features are abroad,
I am skill-less of; but, by my modesty,
The jewel in my dower, I would not wish
Any companion in the world but you,
Nor can imagination form a shape,
Besides yourself, to like of. But I prattle
Something too wildly and my father's precepts
I therein do forget.

Fer.   I am in my condition
A prince, Miranda; I do think, a king;   6c
I would, not so!—and would no more endure
This wooden slavery than to suffer

The flesh-fly blow my mouth.   Hear my soul speak:
The very instant that I saw you, did
My heart fly to your service; there resides,
To make me slave to it; and for your sake
Am I this patient log-man.

    Mir.   Do you love me?

    Fer. O heaven, O earth, bear witness to this sound
And crown what I profess with kind event
If I speak true! if hollowly, invert   70
What best is boded me to mischief!   I
Beyond all limit of what else i' the world
Do love, prize, honour you.

    Mir.   I am a fool
To weep at what I am glad of.

    Pros.   Fair encounter
Of two most rare affections!   Heavens rain grace
On that which breeds between 'em!

    Fer.   Wherefore weep you?

    Mir. At mine unworthiness that dare not offer
What I desire to give, and much less take
What I shall die to want.   But this is trifling;
And all the more it seeks to hide itself,   80
The bigger bulk it shows.   Hence, bashful cunning!
And prompt me, plain and holy innocence!
I am your wife, if you will marry me;
If not, I'll die your maid: to be your fellow
You may deny me; but I'll be your servant,
Whether you will or no.

    Fer.   My mistress, dearest;
And I thus humble ever.

    Mir.   My husband, then?

    Fer.   Ay, with a heart as willing
As bondage e'er of freedom: here's my hand.

    Mir. And mine, with my heart in't: and now farewell 90
Till half an hour hence.

Fer.   A thousand thousand!
                    [*Exeunt Fer. and Mir. severally.*
Pros. So glad of this as they I cannot be,
Who are surprised withal; but my rejoicing
At nothing can be more.   I 'll to my book,
For yet ere supper-time must I perform
Much business appertaining.   [*Exit.*

SCENE II.   *Another part of the island.*

Enter CALIBAN, STEPHANO, *and* TRINCULO.

Ste. Tell not me; when the butt is out, we will drink water;
not a drop before: therefore bear up, and board 'em.   Servant-
monster, drink to me.

Trin. Servant-monster! the folly of this island!   They
say there 's but five upon this isle: we are three of them;
if th' other two be brained like us, the state totters.

Ste. Drink, servant-monster, when I bid thee: thy eyes
are almost set in thy head.

Trin. Where should they be set else? he were a brave
monster indeed, if they were set in his tail.   10

Ste. My man-monster hath drown'd his tongue in sack: for
my part, the sea cannot drown me; I swam, ere I could recover the shore, five and thirty leagues off and on.   By this
light, thou shalt be my lieutenant, monster, or my standard.

Trin. Your lieutenant, if you list; he 's no standard.

Ste. We 'll not run, Monsieur Monster.

Trin. Nor go neither; but you 'll lie like dogs and yet
say nothing neither.

Ste. Moon-calf, speak once in thy life, if thou beest a good
moon-calf.   20

Cal. How does thy honour?   Let me lick thy shoe.
I 'll not serve him; he is not valiant.

Trin. Thou liest, most ignorant monster: I am in case to

justle a constable. Why, thou deboshed fish, thou, was there ever man a coward that hath drunk so much sack as I to-day? Wilt thou tell a monstrous lie, being but half a fish and half a monster?

Cal. Lo, how he mocks me! wilt thou let him, my lord?

Trin. 'Lord' quoth he! That a monster should be such a natural!

30

Cal. Lo, lo, again! bite him to death, I prithee.

Ste. Trinculo, keep a good tongue in your head: if you prove a mutineer,—the next tree! The poor monster's my subject and he shall not suffer indignity.

Cal. I thank my noble lord. Wilt thou be pleased to hearken once again to the suit I made to thee?

Ste. Marry, will I: kneel and repeat it; I will stand, and so shall Trinculo.

Enter ARIEL, *invisible.*

Cal. As I told thee before, I am subject to a tyrant, a sorcerer, that by his cunning hath cheated me of the island.

Ari. Thou liest.

41

Cal. Thou liest, thou jesting monkey, thou:
I would my valiant master would destroy thee!
I do not lie.

Ste. Trinculo, if you trouble him any more in's tale, by this hand, I will supplant some of your teeth.

Trin. Why, I said nothing.

Ste. Mum, then, and no more. Proceed.

Cal. I say, by sorcery he got this isle;
From me he got it. If thy greatness will
Revenge it on him,—for I know thou darest,
But this thing dare not,—

50

Ste. That's most certain.

Cal. Thou shalt be lord of it and I'll serve thee.

Ste. How now shall this be compassed? Canst thou bring me to the party?

Cal. Yea, yea, my lord: I'll yield him thee asleep,
Where thou mayst knock a nail into his head.

Ari. Thou liest; thou canst not.

Cal. What a pied ninny's this! Thou scurvy patch! 60
I do beseech thy greatness, give him blows
And take his bottle from him: when that's gone
He shall drink nought but brine; for I'll not show him
Where the quick freshes are.

Ste. Trinculo, run into no further danger: interrupt the
monster one word further, and, by this hand, I'll turn my
mercy out o' doors and make a stock-fish of thee.

Trin. Why, what did I? I did nothing. I'll go farther
off.

Ste. Didst thou not say he lied? 70

Ari. Thou liest.

Ste. Do I so? take thou that. [*Beats Trin.*]
As you like this, give me the lie another time.

Trin. I did not give the lie. Out o' your wits and hearing
too? A pox o' your bottle! this can sack and drinking do.
A murrain on your monster, and the devil take your fingers!

Cal. Ha, ha, ha!

Ste. Now, forward with your tale. Prithee, stand farther
off.

Cal. Beat him enough: after a little time 80
I'll beat him too.

Ste. Stand farther. Come, proceed.

Cal. Why, as I told thee, 'tis a custom with him,
I' th' afternoon to sleep: there thou mayst brain him,
Having first seized his books, or with a log
Batter his skull, or paunch him with a stake,
Or cut his wezand with thy knife. Remember
First to possess his books; for without them
He's but a sot, as I am, nor hath not
One spirit to command: they all do hate him
As rootedly as I. Burn but his books. 90

He has brave utensils,—for so he calls them,—
Which, when he has a house, he'll deck withal.
And that most deeply to consider is
The beauty of his daughter; he himself
Calls her a nonpareil: I never saw a woman,
But only Sycorax my dam and she;
But she as far surpasseth Sycorax
As great'st does least.

  Ste.   Is it so brave a lass?

  Cal. Ay, lord.   99

  Ste. Monster, I will kill this man: his daughter and I
will be king and queen,—save our graces!—and Trinculo
and thyself shall be viceroys. Dost thou like the plot,
Trinculo?

  Trin. Excellent.

  Ste. Give me thy hand: I am sorry I beat thee; but, while
thou livest, keep a good tongue in thy head.

  Cal. Within this half hour will he be asleep:
Wilt thou destroy him then?

  Ste.   Ay, on mine honour.

  Ari. This will I tell my master.

  Cal. Thou makest me merry; I am full of pleasure: 110
Let us be jocund: will you troll the catch
You taught me but while-ere?

  Ste. At thy request, monster, I will do reason, any reason.
Come on, Trinculo, let us sing.   [*Sings.*

      Flout 'em and scout 'em
      And scout 'em and flout 'em;
       Thought is free.

  Cal. That's not the tune.
      [*Ariel plays the tune on a tabor and pipe.*
  Ste. What is this same?

  Trin. This is the tune of our catch, played by the picture
of Nobody.   121

Ste. If thou beest a man, show thyself in thy likeness: if thou beest a devil, take 't as thou list.

Trin. O, forgive me my sins!

Ste. He that dies pays all debts: I defy thee. Mercy upon us!

Cal. Art thou afeard?

Ste. No, monster, not I.

Cal. Be not afeard: the isle is full of noises,
Sounds and sweet airs, that give delight and hurt not.   130
Sometimes a thousand twangling instruments
Will hum about mine ears, and sometime voices
That, if I then had waked after long sleep,
Will make me sleep again: and then, in dreaming,
The clouds methought would open and show riches
Ready to drop upon me, that, when I waked,
I cried to dream again.

Ste. This will prove a brave kingdom to me, where I shall
have my music for nothing.

Cal. When Prospero is destroyed.   140

Ste. That shall be by and by: I remember the story.

Trin. The sound is going away; let 's follow it, and after do our work.

Ste. Lead, monster; we 'll follow. I would I could see this taborer; he lays it on.

Trin. Wilt come? I 'll follow, Stephano.   [*Exeunt.*

SCENE III. *Another part of the island.*

Enter ALONSO, SEBASTIAN, ANTONIO, GONZALO, ADRIAN, FRANCISCO, *and others.*

Gon. By 'r lakin, I can go no further, sir;
My old bones ache: here 's a maze trod indeed
Through forth-rights and meanders! By your patience,
I needs must rest me.

Alon.   Old lord, I cannot blame thee,
Who am myself attach'd with weariness,
To the dulling of my spirits: sit down, and rest.
Even here I will put off my hope and keep it
No longer for my flatterer: he is drown'd
Whom thus we stray to find, and the sea mocks
Our frustrate search on land.   Well, let him go.   10
    Ant. [*Aside to Seb.*] I am right glad that he's so out of
      hope.
Do not, for one repulse, forego the purpose
That you resolved to effect.
    Seb.   [*Aside to Ant.*] The next advantage
Will we take throughly.
    Ant.   [*Aside to Seb.*] Let it be to-night;
For, now they are oppress'd with travel, they
Will not, nor cannot, use such vigilance
As when they are fresh.
    Seb.   [*Aside to Ant.*] I say, to-night: no more.
                    [*Solemn and strange music.*
Alon. What harmony is this?   My good friends, hark!
Gon. Marvellous sweet music!

Enter PROSPERO *above, invisible.   Enter several strange
    Shapes, bringing in a banquet; they dance about it with
    gentle actions of salutation; and, inviting the King, &c.,
    to eat, they depart.*

    Alon. Give us kind keepers, heavens!   What were these?
    Seb. A living drollery.   Now I will believe   21
That there are unicorns, that in Arabia
There is one tree, the phœnix' throne, one phœnix
At this hour reigning there.
    Ant.   I'll believe both;
And what does else want credit, come to me,
And I'll be sworn 'tis true: travellers ne'er did lie,
Though fools at home condemn 'em.

   Gon.   If in Naples
I should report this now, would they believe me?
If I should say, I saw such islanders—
For, certes, these are people of the island—   30
Who, though they are of monstrous shape, yet, note,
Their manners are more gentle-kind than of
Our human generation you shall find
Many, nay, almost any.
   Pros.   *[Aside]* Honest lord,
Thou hast said well; for some of you there present
Are worse than devils.
   Alon.   I cannot too much muse
Such shapes, such gesture and such sound, expressing,
Although they want the use of tongue, a kind
Of excellent dumb discourse.
   Pros.   *[Aside]* Praise in departing.
   Fran. They vanish'd strangely.
   Seb.   No matter, since   40
They have left their viands behind; for we have stomachs.
Will 't please you taste of what is here?
   Alon.   Not I.
   Gon. Faith, sir, you need not fear. When we were boys,
Who would believe that there were mountaineers
Dew-lapp'd like bulls, whose throats had hanging at 'em
Wallets of flesh? or that there were such men
Whose heads stood in their breasts? which now we find
Each putter-out of five for one will bring us
Good warrant of.
   Alon.   I will stand to and feed,
Although my last: no matter, since I feel   50
The best is past. Brother, my lord the duke,
Stand to and do as we.

Thunder and lightning. Enter ARIEL, *like a harpy; claps his wings upon the table; and, with a quaint device, the banquet vanishes.*

Ari. You are three men of sin, whom Destiny,
That hath to instrument this lower world
And what is in 't, the never-surfeited sea
Hath caused to belch up you; and on this island
Where man doth not inhabit; you 'mongst men
Being most unfit to live. I have made you mad;
And even with such-like valour men hang and drown
Their proper selves.   [*Alon., Seb., &c., draw their swords.*
             You fools! I and my fellows   60
Are ministers of Fate: the elements,
Of whom your swords are temper'd, may as well
Wound the loud winds, or with bemock'd-at stabs
Kill the still-closing waters, as diminish
One dowle that 's in my plume: my fellow-ministers
Are like invulnerable. If you could hurt,
Your swords are now too massy for your strengths
And will not be uplifted. But remember—
For that 's my business to you—that you three
From Milan did supplant good Prospero;   70
Exposed unto the sea, which hath requit it,
Him and his innocent child: for which foul deed
The powers, delaying, not forgetting, have
Incensed the seas and shores, yea, all the creatures,
Against your peace. Thee of thy son, Alonso,
They have bereft; and do pronounce by me
Lingering perdition, worse than any death
Can be at once, shall step by step attend
You and your ways; whose wraths to guard you from—
Which here, in this most desolate isle, else falls   80
Upon your heads—is nothing but heart-sorrow
And a clear life ensuing.

*He vanishes in thunder; then, to soft music, enter the Shapes
    again, and dance, with mocks and mows, and carrying
    out the table.*

  Pros. Bravely the figure of this harpy hast thou
Perform'd, my Ariel; a grace it had, devouring:
Of my instruction hast thou nothing bated
In what thou hadst to say: so, with good life
And observation strange, my meaner ministers
Their several kinds have done.   My high charms work
And these mine enemies are all knit up
In their distractions; they now are in my power;   90
And in these fits I leave them, while I visit
Young Ferdinand, whom they suppose is drown'd,
And his and mine loved darling.   [*Exit above.*
  Gon. I' the name of something holy, sir, why stand
    you
In this strange stare?
  Alon.   O, it is monstrous, monstrous!
Methought the billows spoke and told me of it;
The winds did sing it to me, and the thunder,
That deep and dreadful organ-pipe, pronounced
The name of Prosper: it did bass my trespass.
Therefore my son i' the ooze is bedded, and   100
I 'll seek him deeper than e'er plummet sounded
And with him there lie mudded.   [*Exit.*
  Seb.   But one fiend at a time,
I 'll fight their legions o'er.
  Ant.   I 'll be thy second.
                         [*Exeunt Seb. and Ant.*
  Gon. All three of them are desperate: their great
    guilt,
Like poison given to work a great time after,
Now 'gins to bite the spirits.   I do beseech you
That are of suppler joints, follow them swiftly

And hinder them from what this ecstasy
May now provoke them to.

  Adr.   Follow, I pray you. [*Exeunt*

ACT IV.

SCENE I. *Before* PROSPERO'S *cell.*

Enter PROSPERO, FERDINAND, *and* MIRANDA.

 Pros. If I have too austerely punish'd you,
Your compensation makes amends, for I
Have given you here a third of mine own life,
Or that for which I live; who once again
I tender to thy hand: all thy vexations
Were but my trials of thy love, and thou
Hast strangely stood the test: here, afore Heaven,
I ratify this my rich gift. O Ferdinand,
Do not smile at me that I boast her off,
For thou shalt find she will outstrip all praise 10
And make it halt behind her.

  Fer.   I do believe it
Against an oracle.

  Pros. Then, as my gift and thine own acquisition
Worthily purchased, take my daughter: but
If thou dost break her virgin-knot before
All sanctimonious ceremonies may
With full and holy rite be minister'd,
No sweet aspersion shall the heavens let fall
To make this contract grow; but barren hate,
Sour-eyed disdain and discord shall bestrew 20
The union of your bed with weeds so loathly
That you shall hate it both: therefore take heed,
As Hymen's lamps shall light you.

Fer.   As I hope
For quiet days, fair issue and long life,
With such love as 't is now, the murkiest den,
The most opportune place, the strong'st suggestion
Our worser genius can, shall never melt
Mine honour into lust, to take away
The edge of that day's celebration
When I shall think or Phœbus' steeds are founder'd,   30
Or Night kept chain'd below.
    Pros.   Fairly spoke.
Sit then and talk with her; she is thine own.
What, Ariel! my industrious servant, Ariel!

Enter ARIEL.

    Ari. What would my potent master? here I am.
    Pros. Thou and thy meaner fellows your last service
Did worthily perform; and I must use you
In such another trick.   Go bring the rabble,
O'er whom I give thee power, here to this place:
Incite them to quick motion; for I must
Bestow upon the eyes of this young couple   40
Some vanity of mine art: it is my promise,
And they expect it from me.
    Ari.   Presently?
    Pros. Ay, with a twink.
    Ari.   Before you can say 'come' and 'go',
             And breathe twice and cry 'so, so',
             Each one, tripping on his toe,
             Will be here with mop and mow.
             Do you love me, master? no?
    Pros. Dearly, my delicate Ariel.   Do not approach
Till thou dost hear me call.
    Ari.   Well, I conceive. [*Exit.* 50
    Pros. Look thou be true; do not give dalliance
Too much the rein: the strongest oaths are straw

To the fire i' the blood: be more abstemious,
Or else, good night your vow!

Fer.   I warrant you, sir;
The white cold virgin snow upon my heart
Abates the ardour of my liver.

Pros.   Well.
Now come, my Ariel! bring a corollary,
Rather than want a spirit: appear, and pertly!
No tongue! all eyes! be silent.   [*Soft music.*

Enter IRIS.

Iris. Ceres, most bounteous lady, thy rich leas   60
Of wheat, rye, barley, vetches, oats and pease;
Thy turfy mountains, where live nibbling sheep,
And flat meads thatch'd with stover, them to keep;
Thy banks with pioned and twilled brims,
Which spongy April at thy hest betrims,
To make cold nymphs chaste crowns; and thy broom-groves,
Whose shadow the dismisséd bachelor loves,
Being lass-lorn; thy pole-clipt vineyard;
And thy sea-marge, sterile and rocky-hard,
Where thou thyself dost air;—the queen o' the sky,   70
Whose watery arch and messenger am I,
Bids thee leave these, and with her sovereign grace,
Here on this grass-plot, in this very place,
To come and sport: her peacocks fly amain:
Approach, rich Ceres, her to entertain.

Enter CERES.

Cer. Hail, many-coloured messenger, that ne'er
Dost disobey the wife of Jupiter;
Who with thy saffron wings upon my flowers
Diffusest honey-drops, refreshing showers,
And with each end of thy blue bow dost crown   80

My bosky acres and my unshrubb'd down,
Rich scarf to my proud earth; why hath thy queen
Summon'd me hither, to this short-grass'd green?

   Iris. A contract of true love to celebrate;
And some donation freely to estate
On the blest lovers.
   Cer.   Tell me, heavenly bow,
If Venus or her son, as thou dost know,
Do now attend the queen? Since they did plot
The means that dusky Dis my daughter got,
Her and her blind boy's scandal'd company   90
I have forsworn.
   Iris.   Of her society
Be not afraid: I met her deity
Cutting the clouds towards Paphos and her son
Dove-drawn with her. Here thought they to have done
Some wanton charm upon this man and maid,
Whose vows are, that no bed-right shall be paid
Till Hymen's torch be lighted: but in vain;
Mars's hot minion is return'd again;
Her waspish-headed son has broke his arrows,
Swears he will shoot no more, but play with sparrows   100
And be a boy right out.
   Cer.   High'st queen of state,
Great Juno, comes; I know her by her gait.

Enter JUNO.

   Juno. How does my bounteous sister? Go with me
To bless this twain, that they may prosperous be
And honour'd in their issue.   [*They sing.*

     Juno. Honour, riches, marriage-blessing,
            Long continuance, and increasing,
            Hourly joys be still upon you!
            Juno sings her blessings on you.

Cer. Earthës increase, foison plenty,   110
　　Barns and garners never empty,
　　Vines with clustering bunches growing,
　　Plants with goodly burthen bowing;

　　Spring come to you at the farthest
　　In the very end of harvest!
　　Scarcity and want shall shun you;
　　Ceres' blessing so is on you.

Fer. This is a most majestic vision, and
Harmonious charmingly.   May I be bold
To think these spirits?
　　Pros.　　　　　Spirits, which by mine art   120
I have from their confines call'd to enact
My present fancies.
　　Fer.　　　　Let me live here ever;
So rare a wonder'd father and a wise
Makes this place Paradise.

　　[*Juno and Ceres whisper, and send Iris on employment.*
　　Pros.　　　　　Sweet, now, silence!
Juno and Ceres whisper seriously;
There 's something else to do: hush, and be mute,
Or else our spell is marr'd.

　　Iris. You nymphs, call'd Naiads, of the windring brooks,
With your sedged crowns and ever-harmless looks,
Leave your crisp channels and on this green land   130
Answer your summons; Juno does command:
Come, temperate nymphs, and help to celebrate
A contract of true love; be not too late.

Enter certain Nymphs.

You sunburnt sicklemen, of August weary,
Come hither from the furrow and be merry:
Make holiday; your rye-straw hats put on

And these fresh nymphs encounter every one
In country footing.

*Enter certain Reapers, properly habited: they join with the
    Nymphs in a graceful dance; towards the end whereof
    PROSPERO starts suddenly, and speaks; after which, to a
    strange, hollow, and confused noise, they heavily vanish.*

   Pros. [*Aside*] I had forgot that foul conspiracy
Of the beast Caliban and his confederates   140
Against my life: the minute of their plot
Is almost come. [*To the Spirits.*] Well done! avoid; no
    more!
   Fer. This is strange: your father's in some passion
That works him strongly.
   Mir.   Never till this day
Saw I him touch'd with anger so distemper'd.
   Pros. You do look, my son, in a moved sort,
As if you were dismay'd: be cheerful, sir.
Our revels now are ended.   These our actors,
As I foretold you, were all spirits and
Are melted into air, into thin air: 150
And, like the baseless fabric of this vision,
The cloud-capp'd towers, the gorgeous palaces,
The solemn temples, the great globe itself,
Yea, all which it inherit, shall dissolve
And, like this insubstantial pageant faded,
Leave not a rack behind.   We are such stuff
As dreams are made on, and our little life
Is rounded with a sleep.   Sir, I am vex'd;
Bear with my weakness; my old brain is troubled:
Be not disturb'd with my infirmity: 160
If you be pleased, retire into my cell
And there repose: a turn or two I'll walk,
To still my beating mind.

Fer. ⎫
Mir. ⎭   We wish your peace.   [*Exeunt.*

Pros. Come with a thought.   I thank thee, Ariel: come.

Enter ARIEL.

Ari. Thy thoughts I cleave to.   What's thy pleasure?
Pros.   Spirit,
We must prepare to meet with Caliban.

Ari. Ay, my commander: when I presented Ceres,
I thought to have told thee of it, but I fear'd
Lest I might anger thee.

Pros. Say again, where didst thou leave these varlets? 170

Ari. I told you, sir, they were red-hot with drinking;
So full of valour that they smote the air
For breathing in their faces; beat the ground
For kissing of their feet; yet always bending
Towards their project.   Then I beat my tabor;
At which, like unback'd colts, they prick'd their ears,
Advanced their eyelids, lifted up their noses
As they smelt music: so I charm'd their ears
That calf-like they my lowing follow'd through
Tooth'd briers, sharp furzes, pricking goss and thorns   180
Which enter'd their frail shins: at last I left them
I' the filthy-mantled pool beyond your cell,
There dancing up to the chins, that the foul lake
O'erstunk their feet.

Pros.   This was well done, my bird.
Thy shape invisible retain thou still:
The trumpery in my house, go bring it hither,
For stale to catch these thieves.

Ari.   I go, I go.   [*Exit.*

Pros. A devil, a born devil, on whose nature
Nurture can never stick; on whom my pains,
Humanely taken, all, all lost, quite lost;   190
And as with age his body uglier grows,

So his mind cankers.　I will plague them all,
Even to roaring.

Re-enter ARIEL, *loaded with glistering apparel, &c.*

Come, hang them on this line.

PROSPERO *and* ARIEL *remain, invisible. Enter* CALIBAN,
STEPHANO, *and* TRINCULO, *all wet.*

Cal. Pray you, tread softly, that the blind mole may not
Hear a foot fall: we now are near his cell.

Ste. Monster, your fairy, which you say is a harmless fairy,
has done little better than played the Jack with us.　Do you
hear, monster?　If I should take a displeasure against you,
look you,—

Trin. Thou wert but a lost monster.　　　　　　　　200

Cal. Good my lord, give me thy favour still.
Be patient, for the prize I'll bring thee to
Shall hoodwink this mischance: therefore speak softly.
All's hush'd as midnight yet.

Trin. Ay, but to lose our bottles in the pool,—

Ste. There is not only disgrace and dishonour in that,
monster, but an infinite loss.

Trin. That's more to me than my wetting: yet this is your
harmless fairy, monster.

Ste. I will fetch off my bottle, though I be o'er ears for my
labour.　　　　　　　　　　　　　　　　　　　211

Cal. Prithee, my king, be quiet.　See'st thou here,
This is the mouth o' the cell: no noise, and enter.
Do that good mischief which may make this island
Thine own for ever, and I, thy Caliban,
For aye thy foot-licker.

Ste. Give me thy hand.　I do begin to have bloody thoughts.

Trin. O king Stephano!　O peer!　O worthy Stephano!
look what a wardrobe here is for thee!

Cal. Let it alone, thou fool; it is but trash.　　　220

Trin. O, ho, monster! we know what belongs to a frippery.
O king Stephano!

Ste. Put off that gown, Trinculo; by this hand, I'll have
that gown.

Trin. Thy grace shall have it.

Cal. The dropsy drown this fool! what do you mean
To dote thus on such luggage?   Let's alone
And do the murder first: if he awake,
From toe to crown he'll fill our skins with pinches,
Make us strange stuff.   230

Ste. Be you quiet, monster.   Mistress line, is not this my
jerkin?   Now is the jerkin under the line: now, jerkin, you
are like to lose your hair and prove a bald jerkin.

Trin. Do, do: we steal by line and level, an't like your
grace.

Ste. I thank thee for that jest; here's a garment for't: wit
shall not go unrewarded while I am king of this country.
'Steal by line and level' is an excellent pass of pate; there's
another garment for't.

Trin. Monster, come, put some lime upon your fingers,
and away with the rest.   241

Cal. I will have none on't: we shall lose our time,
And all be turn'd to barnacles, or to apes
With foreheads villanous low.

Ste. Monster, lay-to your fingers: help to bear this away
where my hogshead of wine is, or I'll turn you out of my
kingdom: go to, carry this.

Trin. And this.

Ste. Ay, and this.

*A noise of hunters heard.   Enter divers Spirits, in shape of
    dogs and hounds, and hunt them about,* PROSPERO *and*
    ARIEL *setting them on.*

Pros. Hey, Mountain, hey!   250

Ari. Silver! there it goes, Silver!

Pros. Fury, Fury! there, Tyrant, there! hark! hark!
    [Cal., Ste., and Trin. are driven out.
Go charge my goblins that they grind their joints
With dry convulsions, shorten up their sinews
With aged cramps, and more pinch-spotted make them
Than pard or cat o' mountain.
 Ari.   Hark, they roar!
 Pros. Let them be hunted soundly. At this hour
Lie at my mercy all mine enemies:
Shortly shall all my labours end, and thou
Shalt have the air at freedom: for a little   260
Follow, and do me service.   *[Exeunt.*

ACT V.

Scene I. *Before* Prospero's *cell.*

Enter Prospero *in his magic robes, and* Ariel.

 Pros. Now does my project gather to a head:
My charms crack not; my spirits obey; and time
Goes upright with his carriage. How's the day?
 Ari. On the sixth hour; at which time, my lord,
You said our work should cease.
 Pros.   I did say so,
When first I raised the tempest. Say, my spirit,
How fares the king and 's followers?
 Ari.   Confined together
In the same fashion as you gave in charge,
Just as you left them; all prisoners, sir,
In the line-grove which weather-fends your cell; 10
They cannot budge till your release. The king,
His brother and yours, abide all three distracted
And the remainder mourning over them,

Brimful of sorrow and dismay; but chiefly
Him that you term'd, sir, 'The good old lord, Gonzalo';
His tears run down his beard, like winter's drops
From eaves of reeds.   Your charm so strongly works 'em
That if you now beheld them, your affections
Would become tender.

    Pros.   Dost thou think so, spirit?

    Ari. Mine would, sir, were I human.

    Pros.   And mine shall.   20
Hast thou, which art but air, a touch, a feeling
Of their afflictions, and shall not myself,
One of their kind, that relish all as sharply,
Passion as they, be kindlier moved than thou art?
Though with their high wrongs I am struck to the quick,
Yet with my nobler reason 'gainst my fury
Do I take part: the rarer action is
In virtue than in vengeance: they being penitent,
The sole drift of my purpose doth extend
Not a frown further.   Go release them, Ariel: 30
My charms I'll break, their senses I'll restore,
And they shall be themselves.

    Ari.   I'll fetch them, sir.   [*Exit.*

    Pros. Ye elves of hills, brooks, standing lakes and groves,
And ye that on the sands with printless foot
Do chase the ebbing Neptune and do fly him
When he comes back; you demi-puppets that
By moonshine do the green sour ringlets make,
Whereof the ewe not bites, and you whose pastime
Is to make midnight mushrooms, that rejoice
To hear the solemn curfew; by whose aid,   40
Weak masters though ye be, I have bedimm'd
The noontide sun, call'd forth the mutinous winds,
And 'twixt the green sea and the azured vault
Set roaring war: to the dread rattling thunder
Have I given fire and rifted Jove's stout oak

With his own bolt; the strong-based promontory
Have I made shake and by the spurs pluck'd up
The pine and cedar: graves at my command
Have waked their sleepers, oped, and let 'em forth
By my so potent art.   But this rough magic   50
I here abjure, and, when I have required
Some heavenly music, which even now I do,
To work mine end upon their senses that
This airy charm is for, I 'll break my staff,
Bury it certain fathoms in the earth,
And deeper than did ever plummet sound
I 'll drown my book.   [*Solemn music.*

Re-enter Ariel *before: then* Alonso, *with a frantic gesture,*
     attended by Gonzalo; Sebastian *and* Antonio *in like*
     manner, attended by Adrian *and* Francisco: *they all*
     enter the circle which Prospero *had made, and there*
     stand charmed; which Prospero *observing, speaks.*

A solemn air and the best comforter
To an unsettled fancy cure thy brains,
Now useless, boil'd within thy skull!   There stand,   60
For you are spell-stopp'd.
Holy Gonzalo, honourable man,
Mine eyes, even sociable to the show of thine,
Fall fellowly drops.   The charm dissolves apace,
And as the morning steals upon the night,
Melting the darkness, so their rising senses
Begin to chase the ignorant fumes that mantle
Their clearer reason.   O good Gonzalo,
My true preserver, and a loyal sir
To him thou follow'st!   I will pay thy graces   70
Home both in word and deed.   Most cruelly
Didst thou, Alonso, use me and my daughter:
Thy brother was a furtherer in the act.
Thou art pinch'd for 't now, Sebastian.   Flesh and blood,

You, brother mine, that entertain'd ambition,
Expell'd remorse and nature; who, with Sebastian,
Whose inward pinches therefore are most strong,
Would here have kill'd your king; I do forgive thee,
Unnatural though thou art.   Their understanding
Begins to swell, and the approaching tide   80
Will shortly fill the reasonable shore
That now lies foul and muddy.   Not one of them
That yet looks on me, or would know me: Ariel,
Fetch me the hat and rapier in my cell:
I will discase me, and myself present
As I was sometime Milan: quickly, spirit;
Thou shalt ere long be free.

> ARIEL *sings and helps to attire him.*
>
> > Where the bee sucks, there suck I:
> > In a cowslip's bell I lie;
> > There I couch when owls do cry.   90
> > On the bat's back I do fly
> > After summer merrily.
> > Merrily, merrily shall I live now
> > Under the blossom that hangs on the bough.

Pros. Why, that's my dainty Ariel!   I shall miss thee:
But yet thou shalt have freedom: so, so, so.
To the king's ship, invisible as thou art:
There shalt thou find the mariners asleep
Under the hatches; the master and the boatswain
Being awake, enforce them to this place,   100
And presently, I prithee.

Ari. I drink the air before me, and return
Or ere your pulse twice beat.   [*Exit.*

Gon. All torment, trouble, wonder and amazement
Inhabits here: some heavenly power guide us
Out of this fearful country!

Pros.   Behold, sir king,

The wrongéd Duke of Milan, Prospero:
For more assurance that a living prince
Does now speak to thee, I embrace thy body;
And to thee and thy company I bid　　　　　　　110
A hearty welcome.

　　Alon.　　　　　　　Whether thou be'st he or no,
Or some enchanted trifle to abuse me,
As late I have been, I not know: thy pulse
Beats as of flesh and blood; and, since I saw thee,
The affliction of my mind amends, with which,
I fear, a madness held me: this must crave,
An if this be at all, a most strange story.
Thy dukedom I resign and do entreat
Thou pardon me my wrongs.　But how should Prospero
Be living and be here?

　　Pros.　　　　　　　First, noble friend,　　　120
Let me embrace thine age, whose honour cannot
Be measured or confined.

　　Gon.　　　　　　　Whether this be
Or be not, I'll not swear.

　　Pros.　　　　　　　You do yet taste
Some subtilties o' the isle, that will not let you
Believe things certain.　Welcome, my friends all!
[*Aside to Seb. and Ant.*] But you, my brace of lords, were I
　　so minded,
I here could pluck his highness' frown upon you
And justify you traitors: at this time
I will tell no tales.

　　Seb.　　[*Aside*] The devil speaks in him.

　　Pros.　　　　　　　　　　　No.
For you, most wicked sir, whom to call brother　　130
Would even infect my mouth, I do forgive
Thy rankest fault; all of them; and require
My dukedom of thee, which perforce, I know,
Thou must restore.

Alon.   If thou be'st Prospero,
Give us particulars of thy preservation;
How thou hast met us here, who three hours since
Were wreck'd upon this shore; where I have lost—
How sharp the point of this remembrance is!—
My dear son Ferdinand.
    Pros.   I am woe for 't, sir.
    Alon. Irreparable is the loss, and patience   140
Says it is past her cure.
    Pros.   I rather think
You have not sought her help, of whose soft grace
For the like loss I have her sovereign aid
And rest myself content.
    Alon.   You the like loss!
    Pros. As great to me as late; and, supportable
To make the dear loss, have I means much weaker
Than you may call to comfort you, for I
Have lost my daughter.
    Alon.   A daughter?
O heavens, that they were living both in Naples,
The king and queen there! that they were, I wish   150
Myself were mudded in that oozy bed
Where my son lies.   When did you lose your daughter?
    Pros. In this last tempest.   I perceive, these lords
At this encounter do so much admire
That they devour their reason and scarce think
Their eyes do offices of truth, their words
Are natural breath: but howsoe'er you have
Been justled from your senses, know for certain
That I am Prospero and that very duke
Which was thrust forth of Milan, who most strangely   160
Upon this shore, where you were wreck'd, was landed,
To be the lord on 't.   No more yet of this;
For 't is a chronicle of day by day,
Not a relation for a breakfast nor

Befitting this first meeting. Welcome, sir;
This cell's my court: here have I few attendants
And subjects none abroad: pray you, look in.
My dukedom since you have given me again,
I will requite you with as good a thing;
At least bring forth a wonder, to content ye   170
As much as me my dukedom.

Here Prospero discovers Ferdinand *and* Miranda *playing at chess.*

Mir. Sweet lord, you play me false.

Fer.   No, my dear'st love,
I would not for the world.

Mir. Yes, for a score of kingdoms you should wrangle,
And I would call it fair play.

Alon.   If this prove
A vision of the Island, one dear son
Shall I twice lose.

Seb.   A most high miracle!

Fer. Though the seas threaten, they are merciful;
I have cursed them without cause.   [*Kneels.*

Alon.   Now all the blessings
Of a glad father compass thee about!   180
Arise, and say how thou camest here.

Mir.   O, wonder!
How many goodly creatures are there here!
How beauteous mankind is! O brave new world,
That has such people in't!

Pros.   'T is new to thee.

Alon. What is this maid with whom thou wast at play?
Your eld'st acquaintance cannot be three hours:
Is she the goddess that hath sever'd us,
And brought us thus together?

Fer.   Sir, she is mortal;
But by immortal Providence she's mine:

I chose her when I could not ask my father　190
For his advice, nor thought I had one.　She
Is daughter to this famous Duke of Milan,
Of whom so often I have heard renown,
But never saw before; of whom I have
Received a second life; and second father
This lady makes him to me.

Alon.　　　　　　　　I am hers:
But, O, how oddly will it sound that I
Must ask my child forgiveness!

Pros.　　　　　　　There, sir, stop:
Let us not burthen our remembrance with
A heaviness that's gone.

Gon.　　　　　　　I have inly wept,　200
Or should have spoke ere this.　Look down, you gods,
And on this couple drop a blessed crown!
For it is you that have chalk'd forth the way
Which brought us hither.

Alon.　　　　　　I say, Amen, Gonzalo!

Gon. Was Milan thrust from Milan, that his issue
Should become kings of Naples?　O, rejoice
Beyond a common joy, and set it down
With gold on lasting pillars: In one voyage
Did Claribel her husband find at Tunis
And Ferdinand, her brother, found a wife　210
Where he himself was lost, Prospero his dukedom
In a poor isle, and all of us ourselves
When no man was his own.

Alon. [*To Fer. and Mir.*] Give me your hands:
Let grief and sorrow still embrace his heart
That doth not wish you joy!

Gon.　　　　　　　Be it so!　Amen!

Re-enter ARIEL, *with the* Master *and* Boatswain *amazedly following.*

O, look, sir, look, sir! here is more of us:
I prophesied, if a gallows were on land,
This fellow could not drown.   Now, blasphemy,
That swear'st grace o'erboard, not an oath on shore?
Hast thou no mouth by land?   What is the news?   220
   Boats. The best news is, that we have safely found
Our king and company; the next, our ship—
Which, but three glasses since, we gave out split—
Is tight and yare and bravely rigg'd as when
We first put out to sea.
   Ari. [*Aside to Pros.*] Sir, all this service
Have I done since I went.
   Pros.   [*Aside to Ari.*] My tricksy spirit!
   Alon. These are not natural events; they strengthen
From strange to stranger.   Say, how came you hither?
   Boats. If I did think, sir, I were well awake,
I 'ld strive to tell you.   We were dead of sleep,   230
And—how we know not—all clapp'd under hatches;
Where but even now with strange and several noises
Of roaring, shrieking, howling, jingling chains,
And moe diversity of sounds, all horrible,
We were awaked; straightway, at liberty;
Where we, in all her trim, freshly beheld
Our royal, good and gallant ship, our master
Capering to eye her: on a trice, so please you,
Even in a dream, were we divided from them
And were brought moping hither.
   Ari.   [*Aside to Pros.*] Was 't well done?   240
   Pros. [*Aside to Ari.*] Bravely, my diligence.   Thou shalt
      be free.
   Alon. This is as strange a maze as e'er men trod;
And there is in this business more than nature

Was ever conduct of: some oracle
Must rectify our knowledge.

Pros.   Sir, my liege,
Do not infest your mind with beating on
The strangeness of this business; at pick'd leisure
Which shall be shortly, single I 'll resolve you,
Which to you shall seem probable, of every
These happen'd accidents; till when, be cheerful   250
And think of each thing well. [*Aside to Ari.*] Come hither,
          spirit:
Set Caliban and his companions free;
Untie the spell. [*Exit Ariel.*] How fares my gracious sir?
There are yet missing of your company
Some few odd lads that you remember not.

Re-enter ARIEL, *driving in* CALIBAN, STEPHANO *and*
          TRINCULO, *in their stolen apparel.*

Ste. Every man shift for all the rest, and let no man take
care for himself; for all is but fortune.   Coragio, bully-
monster, coragio!

Trin. If these be true spies which I wear in my head,
here's a goodly sight.   260

Cal. O Setebos, these be brave spirits indeed!
How fine my master is!   I am afraid
He will chastise me.

Seb.   Ha, ha!
What things are these, my lord Antonio?
Will money buy 'em?

Ant.   Very like; one of them
Is a plain fish, and, no doubt, marketable.

Pros. Mark but the badges of these men, my lords,
Then say if they be true.   This mis-shapen knave,
His mother was a witch, and one so strong
That could control the moon, make flows and ebbs,   270
And deal in her command without her power.

These three have robb'd me; and this demi-devil—
For he's a bastard one—had plotted with them
To take my life.　Two of these fellows you
Must know and own; this thing of darkness I
Acknowledge mine.

Cal.　　　　　　　I shall be pinch'd to death.

Alon. Is not this Stephano, my drunken butler?

Seb. He is drunk now: where had he wine?

Alon. And Trinculo is reeling ripe: where should they
Find this grand liquor that hath gilded 'em?　　　280
How camest thou in this pickle?

Trin. I have been in such a pickle since I saw you last
that, I fear me, will never out of my bones: I shall not fear
fly-blowing.

Seb. Why, how now, Stephano!

Ste. O, touch me not; I am not Stephano, but a cramp.

Pros. You'ld be king o' the isle, sirrah?

Ste. I should have been a sore one then.

Alon. This is a strange thing as e'er I look'd on.

　　　　　　　　　　　　　[*Pointing to Caliban.*

Pros. He is as disproportion'd in his manners　　290
As in his shape.　Go, sirrah, to my cell;
Take with you your companions; as you look
To have my pardon, trim it handsomely.

Cal. Ay, that I will; and I'll be wise hereafter
And seek for grace.　What a thrice-double ass
Was I, to take this drunkard for a god
And worship this dull fool!

Pros.　　　　　　Go to; away!

Alon. Hence, and bestow your luggage where you found
it.

Seb. Or stole it, rather.　[*Exeunt Cal., Ste., and Trin.*

Pros. Sir, I invite your highness and your train　　300
To my poor cell, where you shall take your rest
For this one night; which, part of it, I'll waste

With such discourse as, I not doubt, shall make it
Go quick away; the story of my life
And the particular accidents gone by
Since I came to this isle: and in the morn
I 'll bring you to your ship and so to Naples,
Where I have hope to see the nuptial
Of these our dear-beloved solemnized;
And thence retire me to my Milan, where   310
Every third thought shall be my grave.
　　Alon.   I long
To hear the story of your life, which must
Take the ear strangely.
　　Pros.   I 'll deliver all;
And promise you calm seas, auspicious gales
And sail so expeditious that shall catch
Your royal fleet far off. [*Aside to Ari.*] My Ariel, chick,
That is thy charge: then to the elements
Be free, and fare thou well! Please you, draw near.
　　　　　　　　　　　　　　　　[*Exeunt.*

EPILOGUE

SPOKEN BY PROSPERO.

Now my charms are all o'erthrown,
And what strength I have 's mine own,
Which is most faint: now, 't is true,
I must be here confined by you,
Or sent to Naples. Let me not,
Since I have my dukedom got
And pardon'd the deceiver, dwell
In this bare island by your spell;
But release me from my bands
With the help of your good hands: 10
Gentle breath of yours my sails
Must fill, or else my project fails,

Which was to please.   Now I want
Spirits to enforce, art to enchant,
And my ending is despair,
Unless I be relieved by prayer,
Which pierces so that it assaults
Mercy itself and frees all faults.
As you from crimes would pardon'd be,
Let your indulgence set me free.   20

NOTES

(For words not explained here, see Glossary.)

LIST OF PRINCIPAL REFERENCES AND CONTRACTIONS

Abbott ....Dr. E. Abbott's *Shakespearian Grammar.*
Coleridge.........S. T. Coleridge. *Lectures on Shakespeare.*
Dowden..........Professor Dowden's *Shakspere: His Mind and Art.*
E.E. ....Elizabethan English.
Furness..........H. H. Furness. *Variorum* Edition of *The Tempest.*
F 1, F 2, F 3, F 4..1st, 2nd, 3rd, 4th Folios.
Ff................All the Folios.
König ....G. König. *Der Vers in Shakspere's Dramen.*
M.E. ....Middle English (about 1100–1500).
Md. E............Modern English.
Moulton..........R. G. Moulton. *Shakespeare as a Dramatic Artist.*
O.E..............Old English (Anglo-Saxon).
O.F..............Old French..
Wright ....Aldis Wright's edition of *The Tempest* in the Clarendon Press
Series.

Dramatis Personæ. This list is given in the Ff., where it follows the Epilogue.

Act I.—Scene I.

This opening scene, contrary to Shakespeare's usual practice, throws little light on the subsequent action of the play. It serves merely to transport us from the world of realities to the domain of enchantment. It contains a vivid sketch of naval operations, which proves that Shakespeare was proficient in the details of seamanship. Dr. Johnson asserted that in this dialogue, "perhaps the first example of sailors' language exhibited on the stage, there are, as I have been told by a skilful navigator; some inaccuracies and contradictory orders". But the second Lord Mulgrave communicated to Malone "a most satisfactory refutation" of this criticism, maintaining that this scene "is a very striking instance of the great accuracy of Shakespeare's knowledge in a professional science, the most difficult to attain without the help of experience". Lord Mulgrave's explanations of the successive operations are given below.

Enter a Ship-Master and a Boatswain. Captain John Smith, in his *Accidence for Young Seamen*, 1626, says that "The Master and his mate is to direct the course, command all the saylors for steering, trimming, and sayling the ship. The Boteswaine is to have the charge of all the cordage, tackling, sailes, fids, and marling spikes, needles, twine and saile-cloth, and rigging of the shippe."

3. Good is not used in answer to the Boatswain's question, 'what cheer?' The Master could not speak of the cheer as *good*, when the ship was in danger of running aground. The word expresses satisfaction that the Boatswain is ready to take orders. A similar interjectional use of *good* occurs in line 14: "Nay, good, be patient"; and in line 18: "Good, yet remember whom thou hast aboard". It is probably a contraction of a common form of address, *e.g.* 'Good, my lord'.

3, 4. fall to 't, yarely, or we run ourselves aground. "Land discovered under the lee: the wind blowing too fresh to haul upon a wind with the topsail set. This first command is therefore a notice to be ready to execute any orders quickly" (Mulgrave).

6, 7. master's whistle. In Shakespeare's days a great whistle of gold was the ensign of a naval commander, even of the highest rank. Cf. *Pericles*, iii. 1. 8–10:

> "The seaman's whistle
> Is as a whisper in the ears of death,
> Unheard".

The description of the storm in *Pericles*, iii. 1 should be compared throughout with the present scene.

7. Blow, till thou burst thy wind; addressed to the storm. A similar apostrophe in *Pericles*, iii. 1. 44: "Blow, and split thyself".

if room enough, if there be sea-room enough. "The danger in a good sea-boat is only from being too near the land" (Mulgrave).

9. Play the men, act with spirit.

15, 16. What cares these roarers. When the verb in E.E. precedes a plural subject it is frequently in the singular. "When the subject is as yet future and, as it were, unsettled, the third person singular might be regarded as the normal inflection" (Abbott, § 335, where numerous examples are quoted). A plural nominative is also often followed by a singular verb, which Abbott regards as a survival of the M.E. Northern plural in *es*.

16. roarers. In the language of Shakespeare's time a blustering bully was called a *roarer*. Cf. Massinger, *The Renegado*, i. 3: "A lady to turn roarer, and break glasses".

for the name of king? In this allusion to the contempt of the elements for regal authority we have an anticipation of the problem of the true limits of obedience and service which underlies this play.

To cabin. Notice the contempt of the 'old salt' for the 'land-

lubber', however high his rank.   The boatswain is an extraordinarily
lifelike sketch.   "What a grand old sea-dog is he!   Neither
Smollett, nor Marryat, nor even Fenimore Cooper ever drew a more
graphic character.   In the space of a single page we learn to know
him as thoroughly as though he lived and moved in our presence—
a thorough seaman is he; a fine, hardened, blustering, dogmatic,
domineering old fellow, whose shaggy beard has been outspread in
a hundred tempests, one not apt to spare either himself or his sub-
ordinates in the way of duty" ("Shakespeare a Seaman", *St. James's
Magazine*, July, 1862).

21. work the peace of the present, create peace at this instant.
Of, signifying 'coming from', 'belonging to', when used with time
signifies 'during'.   (Abbott, § 176.)

26–30. An allusion to the proverb, "He that's born to be hanged
needs fear no drowning".

28, 29. the rope of his destiny, the hangman's rope.

31, 32. "The gale increasing, the topmast is struck to take the
weight from aloft, make the ship drift less to leeward, and bear the
mainsail under which the ship is laid to" (Mulgrave).

31. Down with the topmast! strike or lower the topmast down
to the cap.

31, 32. Bring her to try with main-course, keep her close to
the wind with the main-sail.   To 'lie at try' is to keep as close to the
wind as possible.   Cf. Hakluyt's *Voyages*, 1598, I. 277: "And when
the barke had way, we cut the hawser, and so gate the sea to our
friend, and tryed out al that day with our maine-course".

33. they are louder than the weather or our office, they
drown the roaring of the storm and my orders.

42. for drowning, against drowning.   Cf. Abbott, § 154.

44, 45. lay her a-hold...lay her off.   The Boatswain, finding
the effect of the single sail unsatisfactory, and the danger of shipwreck ever more imminent, issues fresh orders: 'Keep her to the
wind as close as possible, set her fore-sail as well as her main-sail, so
as to carry her off to sea again'.

47. must our mouths be cold?   Possibly a contemptuous
reference by the seaman to the chilling effect of prayer at such a
crisis.   Cf. Beaumont and Fletcher, *The Sea Voyage*, i. 1:

"Thou rascal, thou fearful rogue, thou hast been praying.
          .   .   .   .   Is this a time
To discourage our friends with your cold orisons?"

In *The Scornful Lady*, however, the phrase is used simply in the
sense of *being dead*, which it may bear here.

50. merely. See Glossary.

51. wide-chapp'd, with a wide mouth.

51, 52. lie drowning The washing of ten tides. Pirates, in the time of Elizabeth, were hanged on the shore at low-water mark, and left till three tides had washed over them. Antonio declares that for the Boatswain *three* tide-washings are not enough—he deserves ten.

60. long heath, brown furze. The reading of the Ff. has been altered by Hanmer to *ling, heath, broom, furze,* on the ground that the epithets *long* and *brown* are stiff and out of place here. In support of the Ff. reading Furness quotes a passage from Lyte's *Herbal* (1576): "There is in this countrie two kindes of Heath, one of which beareth his flowers alongst the stemmes, and is called *long Heath.* The other bearing his flowers in tutteys or tuftes at the toppes of the branches, the which is called *smal Heath.*" Lyte further speaks of heath growing on mountains that be "drie, hungrie, and barren", and of furze being found "in untoyled places by the way-sides". Furness therefore thinks that "the names of both plants were suggested by the word 'barren' in Gonzalo's wish for "an acre of *barren* ground", and in calling the furze 'brown' an additional hue of desolation is imparted by suggesting that the acre is so barren that even the weeds on it are dried up and discoloured".

61. The wills above, the will of the Powers above.

Scene 2.

With this scene we enter the domain of enchantment, and in lines 1–374 we have, for the most part, a sketch of the ancient history of the wonderful island. As has been mentioned in the Introduction (§ 20), *The Tempest,* being practically in the form of a Classical drama, requires an equivalent for the Classical Prologue, which explains to the audience the events that have produced the crisis with which the play is concerned. Prospero's conversations with Miranda, Ariel, and Caliban fulfil this function admirably. They are models of lucid narrative, heightened by the fresh and vivid touches which dialogue imparts.

1–13. Miranda's opening speech forms a skilful mode of transition from the preceding scene. It describes the storm, not as experienced on sea, but as witnessed from the land, and suggests that instead of being a natural outbreak of elemental fury, it is due to the influence of Prospero's art.

1. your…you. Throughout this dialogue Miranda invariably addresses her father in the 2nd person plural of respect, while he, except in line 17, speaks to her in the 2nd person singular of affection.

5–13. These lines give us the key to Miranda's character, in which tenderness and simple faith in good are throughout the leading notes. Notice her description of the vessel as 'brave' and 'good', and her instinctive confidence that it carried 'noble creatures'.

7. Who follows a neuter antecedent when it is personified, as here, 'in her'.

11. or ere. The phrase is really pleonastic. *Or* represents E.E. *ær*, 'before'. As this meaning of *or* died out, it seems to have been combined with *ere* for the sake of emphasis. Cf. Abbott, § 131.

13. fraughting souls, the souls who composed the fraught or freight.

14. piteous, pitying.

15. O, woe the day! Miranda, when she speaks these words, supposes not that the crew has escaped, but that her father counts their destruction 'no harm'.

19. Of whence. For this redundant phrase cf. Abbott, § 179.

more better. The double comparative is frequently used by Shakespeare. Cf. Abbott, § 11.

20. full, completely.

25. Lie there, my art. Steevens quotes in illustration Fuller's anecdote about Lord Burleigh, Elizabeth's Lord Treasurer, who, "when he put off his gown at night, used to say, 'Lie there, Lord Treasurer'". Voss aptly notices that "Shakespeare here very skilfully separates Prospero, the man, from Prospero, the magician. A magician, devoted body and soul to his art, can claim but little of our sympathy. . . . But Prospero's magic resides only in his mantle, staff, and book. Prospero himself remains akin to us."

26. wreck. The Ff. here, and in lines 389, 413, 487, read *wracke*, which gives a far finer rhythm.

27. The very virtue of compassion, the very essence of compassion.

29-31. no soul...vessel. There is no necessity to alter the reading of the Ff.; the sense is clear, though grammatically there is an *anacoluthon*. Prospero begins to declare that no soul on board has been lost, but, before completing the sentence, he breaks off into the more emphatic assertion that not so much harm as a hair has befallen any one.

31. Betid, happened. For other examples of the omission of *ed* in the past indicative and past participle after *d* and *t* cf. Abbott, §§ 341 and 342.

32. Which...which. The first *which* refers to 'creature', the second to 'vessel'.

35. inquisition, inquiry.

41. Out, completely.

50. backward. For a similar example of an adverb used as a noun cf. Sonnet cxxviii.:

"To kiss the tender inward of thy hand".

53. Twelve year. For the use of the noun in the singular cf. *2 Henry IV.*, iii. 2. 224: "That's fifty-five year ago". Walker, Abbott, and Wright assert that the first *year* in this line is to be pronounced as a dissyllable, because it is more emphatic than the second. But the preferable scansion is that of Coleridge, Guest, and Furness:

" Twelve | year | since, | Miran | da, twelve | year since ".

The emphasis at the beginning of the line is not on *year* but on *twelve*, and this is indicated by the speaker's voice pausing on the word. Cf. Prosody, § 2.

56. piece, a perfect specimen.

57–59. This is the reading of the Ff., with the omission of a semicolon after *princess*, and is to be interpreted: 'Thy father was Duke of Milan, and his only heir and princess had no meaner descent than this'. Many editors adopt Pope's conjecture of *a princess* instead of *and princess*, but it is unnecessary.

63, 64. It is characteristic of Miranda that she does not mourn over the loss of her royal position, but merely over the sorrow that, as she thinks, she has caused her father during his wanderings.

65. from. For this use of *from* in the sense of 'away from', 'apart from', cf. Abbott, § 158.

Please you, if it please you.

66–87. Prospero's speech here contains a complicated series of *anacolutha*. He begins with the intention of saying, 'My brother received the government of my state from me, whilst I was engaged in the study of liberal arts'. He first inserts the short parenthesis, "I pray thee...perfidious", and then takes up the subject of the sentence again in "he" (l. 68); this is followed by the involved series of relatival clauses, "whom next thyself...Without a parallel" (ll. 68–74); at the end of these Prospero has forgotten the beginning of his sentence, and starts a fresh main sentence in which 'I' is subject, and "brother" is reintroduced as the accusative after "cast upon". Finally, in l. 77, "Thy false uncle" takes up again the original subject, "My brother and thy uncle", and finds its verb in "created" in l. 81.

70. as at that time, then. For this use of *as*, corresponding to the German *als* in *alsdann*, cf. the Collect for Christmas-day: "Almighty God Who hast given us Thy only-begotten Son to take our nature upon Him, and *as at this time* to be born of a pure Virgin". Cf. too Chaucer's *Legende of Goode Women*, 1491: "Us nedeth trewely Nothing *as now*".

80. who. For other examples of the use of the relative in the nominative where we should expect the accusative, cf. Abbott, § 274.

81. trash for over-topping, a mixture of metaphors from hunting and gardening. To *trash* is to fasten a weight on the neck of a dog to prevent him outrunning his companions. Cf. *Othello*, ii. 1. 312, 313:

"If this poor trash of Venice, whom I trash
For his quick hunting".

Overtopping is used of a tree that grows higher than its companions. Cf. *Antony and Cleopatra*, iv. 12. 23, 24: "this pine is bark'd, That overtopp'd them all".

82, 83. or...Or, either...or.

83. key. There is probably a play on two senses of the word: (1) the keys of office, (2) the key for tuning a musical instrument. The latter signification suggests the words that follow.

85. that, so that.

87. on 't, of it.

90. closeness, secrecy, retirement.

91, 92. 'By what, except that it involved such retirement, surpassed in value all popular estimation.'

94, 95. This alludes to the proverb that a father above the common rate of men has usually a son below it.

95. in its contrary, in its opposite nature. Wright mentions that there are ten instances in Shakespeare's works of this form of the neuter possessive pronoun. It does not occur in the Authorized Version of the Bible, 1611.

97. lorded, raised to the dignity of a lord.

98. revenue: accented on the second syllable.

99–102. like one...own lie. The general meaning of this passage is clear: 'Like one who, by repeating a lie, has made his memory such a sinner against truth that he has come to believe his own invention'. (Malone compares Bacon's account of Perkin Warbeck in his *History of Henry VII.*: "Nay himself, with long and continual counterfeiting, and with oft telling a lie, was turned by habit almost into the thing he seemed to be, and from a liar to a believer".) The construction, however, presents great difficulty. If the reading of the Ff. be retained, as in the present text, there is much plausibility in Philpott's interpretation: 'Who having, by telling of it, credited his own lie into truth, making thereby a sinner of his memory'. This sentence would naturally have run, 'Who having into truth, by telling of it, credited his own lie'; but the words "made such a sinner of his memory", which should have been parenthetical, attracted 'credited' into 'to credit', to suit themselves. Furnivall ingeniously suggests that 'having into truth' means 'cutting into, attacking truth'; the passage would then run: 'like one who, garbling truth by repetition of this garbled version, made such a sinner', &c. Most critics adopt Warburton's emendation, 'unto truth', which depends on 'sinner' in the following line, but it is very doubtful whether the change is necessary.

103. out o' the substitution, by reason of being my deputy.

104. executing the outward face of royalty, performing the external duties of a king.

107–109. 'To have no overshadowing barrier between the rôle that he was playing, and the actual office of Duke, he was determined to become complete sovereign of Milan.'

109. **Me**, for me. For omission of the preposition before the indirect object cf. Abbott, § 201.

112. **dry**, thirsty.

117. **his condition and the event**, the terms he made, and the consequences.

118. **might**, here used in the sense of *could*. For other instances cf. Abbott, § 312.

119. **but nobly**, otherwise than nobly.

122. **hearkens**, listens to.

125. **presently**, immediately.

128. **levied**, being levied.

129. **Fated**, suited by destiny.

134. **Will cry it**. The *it* here is probably used indefinitely, as in l. 379: "Foot it featly". It may, however, possibly stand for "my crying" understood from the previous line.

134, 135. **a hint That wrings mine eyes to 't**, a theme that forces tears from my eyes. For this use of *hint* cf. ii. i. 3, 4: "Our hint of woe Is common".

137. **the which**. This use of *the* before *which* is frequent in Shakespeare. "The question may arise why *the* is attached to *which* and not to *who*....The answer is that *who* is considered definite already, and stands for a noun, while *which* is considered an indefinite adjective; just as in French we have '*le*quel' and not '*le*qui'." Abbott, § 270.

144. **In few**, *i.e.* words.

146. **butt**. This, the reading of the first three Ff., is, without doubt, the right one. Had Shakespeare written "boat" (as Rowe conjectured) it would not have been corrupted into the more unusual word. It is evident, however, that *butt* cannot here have its modern meaning of 'cask', as there would be no sense in the words, "not rigg'd, Nor tackle, sail, nor mast". Brinsley Nicholson suggests that it is a nautical term, borrowed by Shakespeare from an Italian original to give local colouring to the tale, and that it may be a version of *Botto*, a sort of sloop with very rounded ribs, very little run, and flattish bottom.

147. **tackle**, ropes. See Glossary.

148. **have**. For a similar change from past to present tense see l. 205.

quit...hoist. See note on *betid*, line 31.

155. **deck'd**. This word, as used here, is probably connected

with the North-country phrase, to *deck* or *deg*, *i.e.* to sprinkle. The sprinkling of clothes before ironing them is known as *degging*.

156. which, referring to "Thou didst smile", l. 153.

157. undergoing stomach, enduring resolution. For this use of *undergoing* cf. iii. I. 2, 3: "some kinds of baseness Are nobly undergone". For a similar use of *stomach* cf. *Henry V.*, iv. 3. 35, 36:

> "That he which hath no stomach to this fight
> Let him depart".

162. who is redundant.

165. have steaded much, have been of much service.

169. But ever, but at any time.

Now I arise. The words are evidently used in their literal sense, as is shown by Prospero in the next line telling Miranda, who is rising on seeing him rise, to "sit still", *i.e.* probably 'keep sitting', not 'sit quietly'. Why Prospero should mention the fact of his rising is not very obvious, but nothing is gained by giving the phrase a symbolic interpretation, *e.g.* 'I arrive at the climax of my story', or 'I reach the crisis of my fortunes'. The stage-direction 'Resumes his mantle' was added by Dyce, and has no warrant in the Ff.

172. more profit, gain greater advantages.

173. princesses. The reading of the first three Ff. is *princesse*, the fourth having 'princess'. The form is probably an abbreviation of 'princesses' according to the custom that words terminating in the sound of *s* may be regarded by the ear as a plural. Cf. *As You Like It* (1st Folio), i. 2. 175: "The *Princesse* cals for you", whereto Orlando replies: "I attend *them* with all respect and duty"; *cals* is probably a misprint for *call*. Wright compares *Macbeth*, v. i. 29 (F I): "Their *sense* are shut", where *sense* is used for *senses*.

174. hours, here used of the occupations in which hours are spent.

176. beating, working to and fro excitedly.

179. dear lady, auspicious mistress.

180–184. The idea of there being crises in life on which the whole future depends finds expression under a different metaphor in *Julius Caesar*, iv. 3. 218–221:

> "There is a tide in the affairs of men,
>   Which, taken at the flood, leads on to fortune;
>   Omitted, all the voyage of their life
> Is bound in shallows and in miseries".

This theory of crises in our existence is one of the leading elements in the poetry of Robert Browning.

181. zenith is here used in the sense of culminating point of fortune.

185. **dulness,** sleepiness.

186. **And** appears to be used to mark the consequence, and is almost equivalent to 'therefore' or 'and therefore'. Wright compares *Much Ado About Nothing*, iv. 1. 287:

> "*Beat.* I was about to protest I loved you.
> *Ben.* And do it with all thy heart."

Stage-direction, *Enter Ariel*. It is probable that Ariel's costume resembled that of Jophiel, an airy spirit, in Ben Jonson's Masque, *The Fortunate Isles and their Union*. He is described as attired in "light silks of various colours, with wings of the same, a bright yellow hair, a chaplet of flowers, blue silk stockings, and pumps and gloves, with a silver fan in his hand".

189–237. In the first part of the dialogue between Prospero and Ariel we learn further details about the origin of the storm in the first scene and the fate of the shipwrecked crew.

193. **quality,** either (1) 'professional skill' (cf. *Hamlet*, ii. 2. 451, 452: "give us a taste of your quality"), or (2) 'confederates'.

196. **beak,** the pointed prow.

197. **waist,** the part between the quarter-deck and the fore castle.

198. **I flamed amazement,** I caused amazement by appearing in the form of flame. Moulton quotes this phrase, and "afire with *me*", in l. 212, to support the theory that Ariel belongs to the element of fire as well as of air. In any case Shakespeare was influenced in his description by travellers' tales. Cf. Introduction, § 13, and the following passage, quoted by Capell from Hakluyt's *Voyages* (1598): "I do remember that in the great and boysterous storme of this foule weather, in the night, there came upon the toppe of our maine yarde and maine maste a certaine little light, much like unto the light of a little candle, which the Spaniards called the *Cuerpo Santo*, and saide it was S. Elmo, whom they take to bee the advocate of sailers....This light continued aboord our ship about three houres, flying from maste to maste, and from top to top: and sometime it would be in two places at once." Wright quotes a similar passage from *Purchas* (1625), where it is stated that some think the light to be a spirit.

200. **bowsprit.** F1 reads 'bore-spritt', of which Murray (*New English Dictionary*) gives two other examples.

203. **cracks,** peals.

207. **constant,** self-possessed.

209. **a fever of the mad,** a fever such as madmen feel.

213. **up-staring,** standing on end. Cf. *Julius Cæsar*, iv. 3. 279, 280:

> "Art thou some god, some angel, or some devil,
> That makest my blood cold and my hair to stare?"

(M 344)   8

218. sustaining, that bore them up in the water.

218, 219. not a blemish, But fresher than before, there was not a blemish, but they were fresher than before.

222. cooling of. The verbal noun is naturally followed by *of*, and Shakespeare treats as verbals many cases which we should consider present participles. Cf. Abbott, § 178.

223. odd angle, an angle that has been taken no account of.

224. in this sad knot, sorrowfully folded thus.

229. still-vex'd Bermoothes, the Bermudas constantly harassed by storms. Wright quotes several kindred spellings of the word— "the Bermootha's", from Webster's *Duchess of Malfi*, iii. 2; "Barmotho pigs", from the same writer's *The Devil's Law-case*, iii. 2; and "the Barmoothes", from Fletcher's *Women Pleased*, i. 2.

231. Who. See note on l. 80.

suffer'd labour, toil they have undergone.

232. for, as regards. Abbott, § 149.

237–304. The latter part of the dialogue between Prospero and Ariel enlightens us as to the spirit's previous history, and the reasons why he puts "all his quality" at Prospero's service—yet with an undercurrent of discontent. "We feel that such a state of bondage is almost unnatural to him—yet we see that it is delightful for him to be so employed. It is as if we were to command one of the winds in a different direction to that which nature dictates, or one of the waves, now rising and now sinking, to recede before it bursts upon the shore" (Coleridge).

239, 240. It is somewhat surprising that Prospero, after asking Ariel the time of day, and being informed that it is "Past the mid-season" (*i.e.* past noon), should add at once, as if he had more precise knowledge than his informant, "At least two glasses". Several critics, to get over the difficulty, have transferred "At least two glasses" to Ariel. But the reading of the Ff. is quite comprehensible, if we imagine Prospero, after Ariel's rather vague answer, raising his head and, by scanning the sun, realizing the exact time of day.

240. two glasses, two hours. The 'glass' is with Shakespeare always the hour-glass. Cf. *All's Well that Ends Well*, ii. 1. 168, 169:

> "Or four-and-twenty times the pilot's glass
> Hath told the thievish minutes how they pass".

In the nautical phraseology, however, of Shakespeare's day, the glass was always the *half-hour* glass. See further, v. 1. 223, note.

242. pains, tasks.

243. remember, remind.

244. me, for me, the ethical dative. Cf. Abbott, § 220.

252. think'st it much, reckonest it an important service.

258. Sycorax. Many derivations have been suggested of this name. The most plausible is that of Hales, who regards it as a compound of the Greek σῦς (sow) and κόραξ (raven), and thus a contracted form of Syokorax. "As both sows and ravens are associated with witchcraft and such superstitions, the compound might serve not ill to denominate the foul witch. The mere grossness of the one animal and the supposed malignity of the other may be referred to, and so the name Sycorax be designed to express a horrid mixture of these two characteristics."

envy, here used in its E.E. sense of 'malice'.

261. Argier, the older form of Algiers.

266. for one thing she did. What this one thing was which saved the life of Sycorax we do not know. Boswell supposes that there was some novel on which the plot of *The Tempest* was founded, and that it contained the incident obscurely hinted at here. Charles Lamb suggests that light may be thrown upon the words from a passage in Ogilby's *Accurate Description of Africa*, 1670, which tells how, when Algiers was being besieged by Charles V. in 1541, a witch of the town persuaded the governor not to surrender, by a prophecy that within nine days the siege would be raised and the enemy dispersed; the event took place, as was foretold, and the witch being acknowledged the deliverer of the town was richly remunerated. "Can it be doubted for a moment," asks Lamb, "that the dramatist had come fresh from reading some older narrative of this deliverance of Algiers by a witch, and transferred the merit of the deed to his Sycorax?"

269. blue-eyed. This may refer to (1) the *pupil* of the eye, and denote the "pale-blue, fish-like, malignant eye which is often seen in hag-like women" (Grant White); or (2) the livid colour of the *eyelid*, which was a sign of pregnancy. Wright, who suggests this view, compares Webster's *Duchess of Malfi*, ii. 1: "The fins of her eyelids look most teeming blue".

272. for, because.

274. grand, great.

276. unmitigable, implacable.

277. Into. For the use of *into* "after verbs of rest implying motion" cf. Abbott, § 159.

284. Yes, Caliban her son. Ariel's interruption here is not easy to account for. Possibly, with his thoughts still running on his promised liberty, he has been absent-minded during part of Prospero's speech, but has caught the last words about the island not being at that time honoured with a human shape. He therefore contradicts Prospero, reminding him that Caliban was then on the island, and Prospero, annoyed, retorts, "Dull thing, I say so," *i.e.* "I have already said that Caliban was there". Prospero throughout this part of the dialogue displays an amount of irritability which proves that he has naturally a fiery temper, though, for the most part, he has brought it under control.

297. correspondent, obedient.

298. my spiriting, my offices as a spirit.

301-303. In F1 these lines are printed:

"Go, make thyself like a nymph o' th' sea:
    Be subject to no sight but thine and mine: invisible
    To every eye-ball else".

Malone transferred "be subject" to the end of line 301, which supplies a fifth foot to that line, and gets rid of the redundant foot in 302. The result, however, is not entirely satisfactory, as l. 302, even after the change, is harsh in its rhythm, and the words 'and thine' seem superfluous, as it is ridiculous to order Ariel not to be invisible to *himself*. It is possible that the reading of the later Ff. in l. 301 "like to a nymph" may be correct, and that the passage should run:

"Go, make thyself like to a nymph o' th' sea:
    Be subject to no sight but mine; invisible—".

307. Heaviness, sleepiness.

311. miss, do without. Notice this confession by Prospero, that Caliban's services cannot be dispensed with.

314-316. Thou earth...thou tortoise. On the application of these phrases to Caliban see Introduction, § 21. They are both used of him before his appearance to prepare the audience for the entrance of an uncouth monster.

316. when, an expression of impatience.

321-374. The dialogue of Prospero with Caliban is in designed contrast to that with Ariel. We have seen how the airy spirit requites his benefactor; we now learn how the half-brute monster repays his kindness with curses and constrained service. See further as to the significance of the passage, Introduction, § 22.

321. wicked, probably 'having baneful qualities'. Spenser speaks of 'wicked weed'. The word is probably caught up by Caliban from Prospero's application of it in the previous line to Sycorax.

323. a south-west. Southerly winds were supposed to bear fogs and vapours. Cf. *As You Like It*, iii. 5. 50: "Like foggy south, puffing with wind and rain"; and *Coriolanus*, i. 4. 30: "All the contagion of the south light on you". One critic has ingeniously inferred from Shakespeare's constant disparagement of the south wind that he was "a person of a somewhat relaxed habit of body, and required a bracing air to be in the full enjoyment of health".

323. you...ye. Originally *ye* is nominative, *you* accusative; but the distinction is not observed by Elizabethan authors. *Ye* is often used for *you* where an unaccented syllable is wanted.

326. pen thy breath up, make thee gasp for breath.

urchins, hobgoblins. The meaning of the word is made evident by the connections in which it is used by Shakespeare and other Elizabethan writers, *e.g. Merry Wives*, iv. 4. 49: "Like urchins, ouphes, and fairies". So Reginald Scot in his *Discovery of Witchcraft* speaks of having been frightened in childhood by stories about "spirits, witches, urchins, elves, hags, fairies". An old song, *The Urchins' Dance*, runs as follows:

> "By the moon we sport and play,
> With the night begins our day:
> As we frisk, the dew doth fall,
> Trip it, little urchins, all,
> Lightly as the little bee,
> Two by two, and three by three,
> And about go we, go we".

The word has also the meaning of *hedgehog*, and it is probable that the uncanny, nocturnal habits of this animal came to be attributed to the obsession of fairies, and thence the name itself to be attributed to a class of malicious spirits.

327, 328. 'Shall, during that desolate period of night when they are permitted to work, all practise upon thee.' For this use of *vast* cf. *Hamlet*, i. 2. 198: "In the dead vast and middle of the night". The various orders of spirits were supposed to have certain stated limits of time during which they might be active. Thus in *King Lear*, iii. 4. 121, the foul fiend, Flibbertigibbet, "begins at curfew, and walks till the first cock". The Ghost in *Hamlet* departs at daybreak.

334. Water with berries in 't. Some critics have detected in this a reference to coffee, which was as yet little known in England. But such an interpretation is very doubtful.

339. Cursed be I that did so! the reading of F 1, but the later Ff. read 'Curs'd be I that I did so', which is preferable as throwing the emphasis on *curs'd* instead of *I*.

342. sty, keep pent up as in a sty.

351-362. This speech is assigned by the Ff. to Miranda. Theobald, following Dryden's version, transferred it to Prospero, and the change has been accepted by practically all modern editors. Yet the evidence against the Ff. reading is not entirely conclusive. The passage as a whole certainly suits the lips of Prospero better than those of Miranda, and it is natural that the enchanter, whom Caliban has already admitted to be his teacher, should remind the monster of the instruction that he has bestowed on him. Moreover, Prospero must almost inevitably have taken pains to make Caliban speak be-

fore Miranda was old enough to act as tutor; on the other hand, if
the speech be Miranda's it explains how Caliban had opportunities
of associating with her, which he sought to turn to evil account.
The words "I pitied thee" fall naturally from Miranda, with her
tender heart, and there is possibly a reminiscence of the maiden's
instructions in Caliban's reply to Stephano's claim of having been
'the man i' the moon', ii. 2. 127, 128:

> "I have seen thee in her...*My mistress* show'd me thee".

358. race, hereditary nature.

364. red plague. Cf. *Coriolanus*, iv. 1. 13: "Now the red
pestilence strike all trades in Rome". In *The General Practise of
Physicke*, 1605, three different kinds of plague sore are mentioned:
"Sometimes it is red, otherwhiles yellow, and sometimes black".

rid, despatch, destroy.

365. learning, used here as often in E.E. in the sense of 'teaching'.
In O.E. *leornian* = learn, and *lǣran* = teach, but already in M.E. the
meanings had become to some extent confused.

Hag-seed, son of a hag.

366. thou 'rt best: a confusion of two constructions: 'To thee
it were best', and 'Thou had'st best'.

367. malice, malicious thing.

369. old may either (1) be used in an intensive tense, cf. *Much
Ado About Nothing*, v. 2. 98: "Yonder's old coil at home"; or (2) it
may mean 'Such as age brings on'; cf. iv. 1. 255: "aged cramps".

370. aches, pronounced dissyllabically. In E.E. the noun is
spelt *ache*, and the verb *ake*. This distinction is invariably preserved
in the Ff. The pronunciation of *ache*, like the letter H, is made
clear by an epigram of Heywood, quoted by Wright:

> "H, is worst among letters in the crosse row,
> For if thou finde him other in thine elbow,
> In thine arme, or leg, in any degree,
> In thine head, or teeth, in thy toe or knee,
> Into what place soever H may pike him,
> Where euer you find ache, thou shalt not like him".

373. Setebos. The name was probably taken by Shakespeare
from Eden's *History of Travayle*, 1577, which contains a translation
from the Italian narrative of Antonio Pigafetta, who accompanied
Magellan in his circumnavigation of the globe. He relates that
Magellan "took by deceit" two gigantic Patagonians "by loading
them with presents, and then causing shackles of iron to be put on
their legs, making signs that he would also give them those chains;
but they began to doubt, and when at last they saw how tney were
deceived, they roared like bulls, and called upon their great devil
Setebos to help them".

Stage-direction, *Re-enter Ariel, invisible*. A conventional stage costume was used to indicate invisibility. Henslowe in his diary mentions among the wardrobe of his company, the Lord Admiral's men, "a robe for to go invisible".

376–379. Mr. Gosse has suggested that in these lines we have a reminiscence of the passage in Marlowe's *Hero and Leander*, where Hero describes her watch-tower to her lover as standing

> "Where all is *whist* and still,
> Save that the sea playing on *yellow sand*
> Sends forth a rattling murmur to the land".

377. kiss'd. This was customary at the time before certain dances. Cf. *Henry VIII.*, i. 4. 95, 96:

> "I were unmannerly, to take you out,
> And not to kiss you".

377, 378. If the Ff. punctuation be preserved, as in the text, the American critic Allen's interpretation is probably correct: "The nymphs are formed on the sands for a dance; the waves are converted by the poet's imagination into a crowd of spectators, restless and noisy, until the spectacle shall begin; when the nymphs indicate by taking hands, courtesying to, and kissing partners, that they *are* beginning, the waves are hushed by the signal into silent attention, and thus the nymphs do, *in effect*, kiss the wild waves whist, all though they *actually* kiss, not the *waves*, but each other". Most editors put a comma after *kissed*, and interpret *The wild waves whist* as a parenthesis, 'the wild waves being silent'. Such a parenthesis, however, is awkward in a song, and the Ff. punctuation is preferable. For *whist* in the sense of 'hushed or 'silenced' cf. Spenser, *Faerie Queene*, vii. 7. 59: "So was the Titanesse put down and whist".

379. Foot it featly, dance gracefully.

380. the burthen bear: Pope's emendation of the Ff. reading 'bear the burden'.

381, 382. The Ff. print these lines as the burden of the song, in which case *Hark, hark!* and *The watch-dogs bark* are probably said by the 'sweet sprites', and the double *Bow-wow* is supposed to come from watch-dogs behind the scenes. Capell assigns *Hark, hark!* and *The watch-dogs bark* to Ariel, in which case *Bow-wow* alone forms the burden.

387. waits upon, attends.

389. again, probably used for 'again and again'.

395. fathom: another use of the singular for the plural. Cf. l. 53. The Ff. reading is *fadom*.

398, 399. "Everything about him that is liable to alteration undergoes a change through the action of the sea."

404. ditty: properly the 'words of a song'. Cf. Bacon's *Essays*, xxxviii.: "And the *ditty* high and tragical, not nice or dainty".

remember, commemorate.

405. nor no. For the double negative cf. Abbott, § 406.

407. 'Raise your eyelids with their fringe of lashes.' For this use of *advance* cf. iv. 1. 177: "Advanced their eyelids". For a justification of Prospero's stilted phraseology here, see Coleridge, pp. 144, 145.

413. but, except that.

something, somewhat.

418. It goes on, the plan prospers.

431. A single thing. Ferdinand plays upon the word. He believes that himself and the King of Naples are one and the same person; he therefore uses this epithet with reference to its further sense of 'solitary', and so 'feeble and helpless'.

432. Naples, the King of Naples. Cf. the following line: "myself am Naples".

434. never since at ebb, always since then flooded with tears.

437. And his brave son. There is no further allusion in the play to a son of the Duke of Milan. He may have appeared in some lost source of *The Tempest*, and this accidental reference may have been preserved. Or Shakespeare, as Theobald suggested, may have marked out such a character in his first plan, but on second thoughts found it unnecessary.

The Duke of Milan, Prospero, the rightful Duke.

438. more braver. For the double comparative cf. Abbott, § 11.

440. changed eyes, exchanged loving glances. Cf. *Antony and Cleopatra*, iii. 13. 156, 157:

"To flatter Cæsar, would you mingle eyes
    With one that ties his points?"

442. you have done yourself some wrong, you have injured your honour by asserting what is not the case, *i.e.* that you are King of Naples.

449. both in either's powers. *Both* seems put for 'each', or *either* used for each other. There may, however, be an ellipsis of *each* after *both*—'They are both (each) in either's powers'. Cf. Sonnet cxxxi:

"A thousand groans . . .
    Came (one) on another's neck". (Abbott, § 12.)

456-458. "Miranda's creed seems to be a simple faith in beauty" (Moulton). Her speech, however, is not quite logical. She declares (1) that nothing evil can dwell in such a temple as Ferdinand's body; (2) that if the evil spirit have so fair a mansion, good things will strive to dwell with it. According to her second statement the 'mansion' will be *shared* by 'the ill spirit' and 'Good things', and this contradicts her first statement. To get over the difficulty it has been suggested that (1) *with't* is a misprint for *in't*; or (2) that *with* is used in the sense of *chez*, though no other instance of this is forthcoming.

464. entertainment, treatment.

467. gentle and not fearful. The most natural interpretation of these words is 'harmless and not terrible', in which case "Make not too rash a trial of him" in l. 466 must mean, 'Do not rashly determine to put him to severe tests'. This interpretation best suits Miranda's attitude throughout this episode, in which her anxieties are on behalf of Ferdinand, not of her father. It is possible, however, that *gentle and not fearful* means 'of gentle birth and not a coward', and that therefore Prospero is warned not to 'make too rash a trial of him' by engaging unadvisedly in a duel with him.

468. My foot my tutor! This pregnant phrase may be paraphrased: 'You, Miranda, to instruct me! The foot to lecture the head.' Cf. Lyly's *Euphues*, p. 261: "Then how vaine is it, Euphues (too mylde a worde for so madde a mind), that the foot should neglect his office to correct the face".

472. Beseech, used, like *pray*, without the personal pronoun.

477. there is. Cf. note on i. 1. 15, 16.

479. To the most of men, as compared with the majority.

483. nerves. See Glossary.

487. nor. Used inaccurately where 'and' or 'or' would be in place. The origin of the error is probably a confusion of two constructions. Shakespeare intending perhaps at first to employ some such word as 'heavy', and then substituting 'but light'.

Act II.—Scene I.

This scene enlightens us further as to the character of Prospero's enemies; it shows that Antonio, the arch-traitor, has been merely hardened in villainy by the lapse of years, and that he has found a fit associate in Alonso's brother, Sebastian. The remarks of the pair, throughout the earlier half of the scene, are an unconscious self-revelation. "The prolonged and dull joking of Sebastian in this scene cannot be meant by Shakespeare to be really bright and witty. It is meant to show that the intellectual poverty of the conspirators is as great as their jovial obliquity" (Dowden). We are "shown the tendency in bad men to indulge in scorn and contemptuous expressions, as a mode of getting rid of their own uneasy

feelings of inferiority to the good, and also, by making the good
ridiculous, of rendering the transition of others to wickedness easy"
(Coleridge). We are thus prepared for the iniquitous attempt of
Antonio against the life of his former ally, Alonso, whose suzerainty
he finds burdensome; and the upright (though somewhat prosy)
Gonzalo, whose 'prating' he detests. To make such an attempt at
the moment, when he has been miraculously saved from death, and
to enlist Alonso's brother as an accomplice, is a refinement of villainy.
The foiling of the plot is the first move in Prospero's policy of
'countercheck' against his foes.

1. **Beseech.** See note on i. 2. 472.

2, 3. 'Our escape much more than balances our loss.'

3. **hint.** See note on i. 2. 134, 135.

5, 6. 'The owners of some merchantman, and the merchant who
has shipped cargo in her.' The double use of *merchant* in the same
line, first for 'the vessel' and then for 'the trader', is awkward.

11. **The visitor,** applied derisively by Antonio to Gonzalo, who
is trying to console Alonso after the manner of a visitor to the sick.

15. **tell,** count; O.E. *tellan.* Cf. Milton, *L'Allegro*:

> "Every shepherd tells his tale
> Under the hawthorn in the dale".

Sebastian, carrying on his jest about the watch, implies that each
word of Gonzalo's represents a stroke.

16-20. Gonzalo begins to moralize upon the result of *entertaining*
or 'giving welcome to' every grief that approaches us. Sebastian,
punning upon *entertainer* in its general application and in its special-
ized sense of 'an innkeeper', flippantly suggests that the *entertainer*
gets *a dollar* for his pains. Gonzalo retorts with a play upon *dollar*
and *dolour* (grief).

19. **truer,** more truly; the adjective for the adverb.

21. **wiselier,** comparative form of adverb.

27, 28. **Which, of he or Adrian...begins to crow?** We seem
to have here a mixture of two constructions—'which of the two,
viz. he and Adrian?' and 'which, he or Adrian?' *Of* belongs to
the first construction, and *or* to the second. Cf. *Midsummer-Night's
Dream*, iii. 2. 336, 337:

> "Now follow, if thou darest, to try whose right—
> *Of* thine or mine—is most in Helena".

32. **a laughter.** Antonio proposes this as the wager. It is just
possible, as Ingleby has suggested, that *a laughter* may be "the
cant name for some small coin commonly laid in betting". There
is indeed no evidence in support of such an interpretation, but the
pun involved would harmonize with the verbal quibbling in the rest
of the passage, and would give point to what seems otherwise an

almost meaningless jest. Sebastian accepts the conditions with the usual formula of assent, *a match*. He loses through Adrian being the first to speak, and then bursting out into *Ha, ha, ha*, adds, *So, you're paid*. On Ingleby's hypothesis the jest consists in Sebastian paying Antonio with a *ha, ha, ha*, instead of a *coin*. The Ff. give *So, you're paid* to Antonio, but Theobald's conjecture that the words belong to Sebastian renders the passage more intelligible.

34-52. From Adrian and Gonzalo's description, in spite of Antonio and Sebastian's unmannerly interruptions, we learn what the climate and the scenery of the island are like.

39. He could not miss't. Either (1) he could not avoid introducing *yet*, or (2) he could not do without the island just now, uninhabitable as it is. Cf. Prospero's statement about Caliban, i. 2. **311:** "We cannot miss him". This interpretation is more in keeping with Antonio's character than the former. He is more likely to make a fresh move in the game of repartee than merely to record the success of Sebastian's last stroke.

40, 41. temperance, temperature. In the next line the word is used as a proper name, like Charity.

43. delivered, declared.

50. lush and lusty, luxuriant and fresh.

52. an eye of green, a slight shade of green. *Eye* was used for a small portion of anything. Malone quotes from *A True Declaration of the Estate of the Colonie in Virginia*, 1600: "Not an eye of sturgeon as yet appeared in the river". Sebastian insinuates that the credulous Gonzalo is the *green* spot in the grass.

53. 'He is not far wrong.'

59. glosses. We should more naturally use the singular.

61, 62. It is not very clear why one of Gonzalo's pockets should give the lie to his previous statement. The remark seems chiefly introduced to lead up to the pun in the next line.

70. to their queen. *To* is here used in the sense of 'as' or 'in the capacity of'. Cf. *S. Luke*, iii. 8: "We have Abraham to our father".

71. widow Dido. The reference is to the famous Queen of Carthage, who was one of the favourite heroines of Renaissance poetry. Marlowe and Nash wrote a play about her. The jesting allusion to her as *widow* is probably founded on some ballad of the day.

76. of that, concerning that. Cf. Abbott, § 174.

81. The miraculous harp is that of Amphion, which raised the walls of Thebes, or that of Apollo, which raised the walls of Troy. So Gonzalo's word has raised anew the walls, and the houses also, of ancient Carthage.

88. **Ay.** The Ff. assign this to Gonzalo, but it is preferable to adopt Staunton's conjecture that it is an exclamation uttered by Alonso on awaking from his trance of grief. This would explain Antonio's "Why, in good time", which refers ironically to Alonso's return to consciousness. It explains further why Gonzalo in l. 90 begins to recapitulate to the king the substance of the preceding conversation.

98. Deighton gives the most plausible explanation of the obscure pun in this line: ' You fished a long time before you succeeded in catching that word *sort*. You have repeatedly tried to make out that our garments are as fresh as if they had never been immersed in the sea, and now at last you qualify your assertion by the word *sort*.' In *fished* there is possibly an allusion also to their difficulty in fishing themselves out of the water.

100, 101. 'You force these words into my ears, which are as loath to receive them as the stomach is to take in food that it does not want.'

112, 113. **oar'd Himself**, impelled himself with arms as oars.

114. **shore**, the cliffs on the shore.

118. **that** has for its antecedent *yourself* in the previous line.

121. **Who hath cause to wet the grief on 't.** *Who* may have as its antecedent either *she* or *eye*. If the former, paraphrase: ' Who lost to sight by banishment, though not by death, hath yet cause to fill your eyes with tears ' (Wright). If *eye* be the antecedent, interpret: 'which has cause to give tearful expression to the sorrow for your folly' (Abbott). For other instances of the use of *who*, with a neuter antecedent, cf. Abbott, § 264.

124. **Weigh'd**, hung evenly.

loathness, reluctance.

124, 125. **at Which end o' the beam should bow.** If we preserve this, the Ff. reading, the best explanation is Wright's, that *it*, whose antecedent is the indecision of Claribel described in l. 124, has been omitted, cf. Abbot, § 404. But it is the *beam* of the balance itself that one naturally thinks of as bowing, and Spence's emendation "at which end o 't th' beam should bow" gives excellent sense, with a trifling change in the reading.

129. **the dear'st**, the most acutely felt part. *Dear* is used in E.E. to denote the excess or superlative of that to which it may be applied. Cf. *Hamlet*, i. 2. 182: "Would I had met my dearest foe in heaven".

132. **time**, seasonable time.

136. **cloudy**, gloomy.

137. **plantation.** Gonzalo uses the word in the sense of *colonization*. Cf. Bacon's *Essay of Plantations*. Antonio jestingly interprets it in its ordinary sense.

141–158. Gonzalo's sketch of his imaginary commonwealth is closely modelled on a passage in.Montaigne, book i. c. 30, "of the Caniballes", which Shakespeare had read in Florio's translation: "It is a nation...that hath no kinde of traffike, no knowledge of Letters, no intelligence of numbers, no name of magistrate, nor of politike superioritie; no use of service, of riches or of povertie; no contracts, no successions, no partitions, no occupation but idle; no respect of kinred, but common, no apparell but naturall, no manuring of lands, no vse of wine, corne, or mettle. The very words that import lying, falshood, treason, dissimulations, covetousnes, envie, detraction, and pardon, were never heard of amongst them."

150–152. Gonzalo had begun (l. 139) by supposing himself *king* of the island. But in his enthusiastic description of an ideal commonwealth in which all social obligations and class distinctions are to be abolished, he forgets the basis from which he started, and asserts that there is to be *no sovereignty* on the island. Sebastian and Antonio are quick to rally him on this self-contradiction, and for once they are probably Shakespeare's mouthpiece. For from the early days when he wrote (as is probable) the 'Jack Cade' scenes in *2 Henry VI.* till the end of his career, he is always found ridiculing Utopian or communistic theories. "He who had earned the New Place, and become a landed gentleman by years of irksome toil, did not see that he was bound to share his tenements and lands with his less industrious neighbours. On the contrary he meant to hold them himself by every legal title, and at his decease to hand them down to his daughter, and her sons, and sons' sons" (Dowden).

155. **engine**, instrument of war.

157. **it own.** Cf. note on i. 2. 95, and Abbott, § 228. *It* is "an early provincial form of the old genitive". Cf. *Lear*, i. 4. 235, 236:

"The hedge-sparrow fed the cuckoo so long,
That it had *it* head bit off by *it* young".

162. **Save.** Before this word we must understand 'God', which was probably omitted in the Ff. in deference to the Act i. Jac. 21, against profanity.

164. **nothing,** nonsense.

165, 166. **minister occasion,** offer a cue.

166. **sensible,** sensitive. *Ible* and *able* have often an *active* instead of a *passive* meaning in E.E.

172. **An,** if. Printed *and* in the Ff. Cf. Bacon, *Essay* 23: "They will set an house on fire, *and* it were but to roast their eggs". *And* is, in fact, the more correct spelling, for which *an* has been substituted by an editorial convention. *An* is frequently conjoined with *if*: cf. *Richard II.*, iv. 1. 49: "An if I do not", and Prof. Herford's note *ad loc.*: "*An* is the modern form of the E.E. *and,* 'if', which is probably merely a special usage of the ordinary conjunction 'and'. From being used to introduce a hypothetical sentence, 'and' acquired

itself a hypothetical sense. *An if* is a trace of the process, before that sense had been definitely reached; but in E.E. it is used simply as = if. It survives in the Somersetshire *nif*."

174. would, here used for the conditional 'should'. Cf. Wright's note on the line.

176. a bat-fowling. *a* is the weakened form of the proposition *on*. *Bat-fowling* is explained by Gervase Markham in his *Hunger's Prevention* (1621) quoted by Wright. "For the manner of *Bat-fowling* it may be vsed either with Nettes, or without Nettes: if you use it without Nettes (which indeede is the most common of the two) you shall then proceede in this manner. First, there shall be one to carry the Cresset of fire (as was shewed for the *Lowbell*) then a cer-taine number, as two, three, or foure (according to the greatnesse of your company), and these shall haue poales bound with dry round wispes of hay, straw, or such like stuffe, or else bound with pieces of Linkes, or Hurdes, dipt in Pitch, Rosen, Grease, or any such like matter that will blaze. . . . Then another company shall be armed with long poales, very rough and bushy at the vpper endes, of which the Willow, Byrche, or long Hazell are best, but indeed according as the country will afford so you must be content to take. . . . Thus being prepared, and comming into the Bushy, or rough ground where the haunts of Birds are, you shall then first kindle some of your fiers as halfe, [or a third part, according as your provision is, and then with your other bushy and rough poales you shall beat the Bushes, Trees, and haunts of the Birds to enforce them to rise, which done you shall see the Birds which are raysed to flye and play about the lights and flames of the fier, for it is their nature through their amazed-nesse, and affright at the strangenes of the light and the extreame darknesse round about it, not to depart from it, but as it were almost to scorch their wings in the same, so that those who have the rough bushye poales may (at their pleasures) beat them down with the same, & so take them."

178. adventure my discretion, put my reputation for discre-tion in peril.

180. Halliwell - Phillips interprets this obscure line as follows: "Gonzalo asks them to laugh him to sleep, for he is very drowsy. Antonio replies, 'Go to sleep and hear us laugh', the sound of which laughter, from a little distance, would soothe the drowsy counsellor into slumber. Antonio's speech, by the common idiom of inversion, is equivalent to 'Hear us and go to sleep'." This explanation, how-ever, is far from convincing, and more point is given to the passage if *laugh* is interpreted in the sense of 'laugh at' (cf. "Scoffing his state", *Richard II.*, iii. 2. 163, and "Smile you my speeches?" *King Lear*, ii. 2. 88). Gonzalo thus inquires, 'Will you gentlemen, who are always a-laughing (cf. 166-170), continue to laugh at me, when I am asleep?' Antonio retorts rudely, 'Go to sleep, and then you'll find out whether we are laughing at you or not'.

184. the heavy offer, the offer that brings heaviness or drowsiness.

194–286. "The scene of the intended assassination of Alonso and Gonzalo is an exact counterpart of the scene between Macbeth and his lady, only pitched in a lower key throughout, as designed to be frustrated and concealed, and exhibiting the same profound management in the manner of familiarizing a mind, not immediately recipient, to the suggestion of guilt, by associating the proposed crime with something ludicrous or out of place—something not habitually matter of reverence. By this kind of sophistry the imagination and fancy are first bribed to contemplate the suggested act, and at length to become acquainted with it" (Coleridge).

197. What thou shouldst be, what thou oughtest to be. Cf. Abbott, § 323, for other instances of this use of *should*.

the occasion speaks thee; either 'the opportunity calls to thee' or 'declares what thou mayest be'.

206. wink'st, closest thy eyes.

210. if heed me; for the ellipsis of 'you' cf. Abbott, § 387.

211. Trebles thee o'er, makes thee three times as great as thou art.

standing water, neither ebbing nor flowing, and so ready to be moved in either direction.

214–216. 'If you but knew how you encourage the design even while you mock at it, how in exposing it in its nakedness you clothe it with greater seriousness. Men who let their fortunes ebb do indeed, as you say, most frequently lose themselves in shallows through their own fears and sloth.' For the metaphor cf. *Julius Cæsar*, iv. 3. 218–221, quoted in note on act i. 2. 180–184.

219. proclaim: attracted into the plural by 'eye' and 'cheek'.

220. A matter, an important business, full of meaning.

221. throes, pains.

222–226. The passage may be paraphrased: 'Although this lord with his weak memory (who, when once laid in the ground, shall be as little remembered as he now remembers other things) has here almost persuaded (for he is the very soul of persuasion, and to practise it is his only profession) the king that his son's alive'.

222. this lord. In all probability Gonzalo, who has been the king's chief comforter, though it is Francisco, according to the Ff., who gave the detailed narrative of Ferdinand's escape by his feat of swimming.

226. Professes, practises as a profession; cf. *1 Henry IV.*, v. 2. 91, 92:

> "I thank him, that he cuts me from my tale,
>   For I profess not talking".

232. a wink, here used of an infinitesimal portion of space; more usually of time.

233. But doubt discovery there. If the Ff. reading be retained, either *but doubt* means 'without doubting' or 'cannot' is carried on from the former line, 'cannot but doubt discovery there', *i.e.* is uncertain whether it can find anything at this extreme limit of its vision. Capell reads 'doubts'.

237. Ten leagues beyond man's life. Such a rhetorically exaggerated phrase need not be interpreted too precisely, but Antonio probably means 'ten leagues beyond the point a man could arrive at by travelling all his life'.

238. note, knowledge, intimation.

240. she that—from whom. The Ff. reading, though grammatically pleonastic, is probably correct. Antonio begins this clause, like the three previous ones, with *she that*, and then changes to *from whom*, which makes *that* superfluous. *From whom* is practically equivalent to 'coming from whom'.

241. cast, thrown up by the sea. But the theatrical usage of the word, to 'cast' for a part, suggests 'act' and 'prologue' in the following lines.

242. 'And by the same destiny that cast us ashore we are fated to perform an act.'

243. prologue. Many plays in Shakespeare's time were preceded by a prologue. Cf. the workmen's play in *A Midsummer-Night's Dream* and the play-scene in *Hamlet*. For the same theatrical metaphor see *Macbeth*, i. 3. 127–129:

> "Two truths are told,
> As happy prologues to the swelling act
> Of the imperial theme".

243, 244. what to come In yours and my discharge, what is to come lies with us to perform. *Discharge* is another theatrical term. Cf. *Midsummer-Night's Dream*, i. 2. 95: "I will discharge it [the part of Pyramus] in either your straw-colour beard,...or your French-crown-colour beard".

249. Keep. By an abrupt change of construction Claribel is directly addressed by "every cubit", instead of being referred to in the third person as "that Claribel", as in the previous line.

255, 256. could make A chough of as deep chat, could teach a red-legged crow to talk as profoundly. Cf. *All's Well that Ends Well*, iv. I. 22, 23: "chough's language, gabble enough, and good enough".

260. Tender, regard.

264. fellows, companions.

267. 'T would put me to my slipper, it would make me have to wear a slipper instead of boot.

269. **candied**, congealed. Cf. *Timon of Athens*, iv. 3. 225–227:

> "will the cold brook,
> Candied with ice, caudle thy morning taste,
> To cure thy o'er-night's surfeit?"

Preserving the Ff. reading, we may interpret the passage: 'Let twenty consciences, that bar my way to the throne of Milan, be frozen or be melted into insensibility before they cause me a twinge'. In this case *melt* is the past participle for 'melted'. Cf. note on i. 2. 31. Upton proposed to read 'discandied', from 'discandy', which is used as equivalent to 'melt' in *Antony and Cleopatra*, iv. 12. 20–23:

> "The hearts
> ...discandy, melt their sweets
> On blossoming Cæsar".

273. **Whom**, referring to *brother* in l. 270.

275. **perpetual wink**, the everlasting sleep, or closing of eyes. Cf. l. 206.

276. **morsel**, here applied contemptuously by Antonio to Gonzalo. For a somewhat similar use of the word Wright compares *Measure for Measure*, iii. 2. 56, 57: "How doth my dear morsel, thy mistress?"

277. **Should not**, would not in that case. Cf. *Troilus and Cressida*, i. 3. 115, 116:

> "the rude son should strike his father dead:
> Force should be right".

Cf. Abbott, § 322.

278. **suggestion**, prompting, temptation. Cf. Sonnet cxliv.:

> "Two loves I have of comfort and despair,
> Which like two spirits do suggest me still".

279. **tell the clock**, count the strokes of the clock. Cf. note on l. 15.

286. **fall it**, let it fall. Cf. Abbott, § 291.

288. **you, his friend.** 289. **them.** The abrupt change from the second person singular to the third plural has led some critics to adopt 'thee' instead of *them*. But this is unnecessary. "Ariel soliloquizes, and is reviewing what he has to do. Gonzalo, the especial friend, is in imminent danger, and must be at once protected; and all of them must be kept alive, just as he had saved them in the tempest when not a hair perished" (Furness).

296. **sudden**, speedy.

298, 299. **Why, how now?...ghastly looking?** Staunton, from a comparison of these lines with 317–322, assigned them to Gonzalo, and transferred "What's the matter?" to Alonso. Dyce adopts this emendation, and adds the following stage-directions:

> "*Gon.* [*waking*].   Now, good angels
> Preserve the king. [*To Seb. and Ant.*] Why, how now! [*To Alon.*]
> Ho! awake!—

[*To Seb. and Ant.*] Why are you drawn?   Wherefore this ghastly
  looking?
  Alon. [*waking*].   What 's the matter?"

300. securing, guarding.

309. shaked.   For this weak form of the past tense instead of
the strong 'shook', cf. *I Henry IV.*, iii. 1. 16, 17:

> "The frame and huge foundation of the earth
>   Shaked like a coward".

311. That 's verily.   For this use of an adverb instead of an
adjective cf. Abbott, § 78.

Scene 2.

This scene opens the comic underplot of the play.   Caliban, who
has hitherto been seen in contrast with humanity in its highest
development, is now brought into contact with the dregs of civilized
society in the persons of Stephano and Trinculo.   Stephano's 'bottle'
wins from the savage the ready allegiance which Prospero's nobler
gifts had failed to obtain.   Yet the 'very shallow monster', with his
perverted instinct of adoration and his rude poetic sense, is felt to
be superior to the drunken butler and jester with whom he forms a
league against the 'tyrant' Prospero.   The conspiracy, hallowed by
Caliban's impassioned Ode to Liberty, is the burlesque counterpart
of the conspiracy in the previous scene.

5. urchin-shows, apparitions of goblins.   Cf. note on i. 2. 326,
and for the use of *urchin* as an adjective cf. Milton's *Comus*, 845,
'urchin blasts'.

9. Sometime, sometimes.

10. after, afterwards.

11. my barefoot way, the way in which I walk barefoot.

  mount, raise.

13. wound, twisted around by.

15. and, and that too.   For this emphatic use of *and* cf. Abbott,
§ 96.

18. bear off, a pregnant phrase, equivalent to ' bear and so keep
off me '.

21. bombard, a large vessel for holding liquor.   Halliwell-
Phillips quotes the following notice of them from Heywood's *Philo-
cothonista*, 1635 : "Other bottles wee have of leather, but they are
most used amongst the shepheards and harvest people of the countrey;
small jacks wee have in many ale-houses of the Citie and suburbs,
tipt with silver, besides the great black-jacks and bumbards at the
Court, which, when the Frenchmen first saw, they reported, at their
returne into their countrey, that the Englishmen used to drinke out of

their bootes". In *1 Henry IV.*, ii. 4. 496, 497, Falstaff is called "that huge bombard of sack". The word is derived from O.F. *bombarde*, and is used by Lydgate, Caxton, and others for 'a cannon' throwing a stone-ball or large shot. Thence applied to a vessel for liquor on account of some resemblance to an early cannon.

27, 28. this fish painted, a painting made of this fish. Trinculo's ideal of art is evidently a daub on a board hung out before a booth at a fair.

29. make a man, make a man's fortune.

30. doit, the smallest coin. Coryat, in his *Crudities*, says that "eight doits go to a stiver, and ten stivers do make one English shilling".

31, 32. a dead Indian. Various commentators have attempted the hopeless task of identifying the savage whose body was thus exhibited. Doubtless many of the Elizabethan seamen brought home 'natives' on board their ships. Thus Frobisher, on his first voyage, 1586, took captive an Indian who "for very choler and disdain, bit his tong in twaine within his mouth; notwithstanding he died not thereof, but lived till he came in Englande and then he died of colde which he had taken at sea".

35. suffered, suffered death. Cf. "suffered under Pontius Pilate" in the Apostles' Creed.

38. shroud, hide.

38, 39. the dregs of the storm. Trinculo is still keeping up the image of the bombard full of liquor. He will hide until the very last drops of the storm are past.

40–51. "Stephano sings a certain jolly sea-song. Hearken to the shrewd and diverting knave as he trolls away, bottle in hand, and monarch of all he surveys. There's good stuff in that song; the writer must have smelt salt water; snuffed the sea-breeze with a hearty reiish, and often had his jacket wetted with the spray" (*Shakespeare a Seaman*, St. *James's Magazine*, July, 1862). The song, in itself, scarcely warrants so confident an inference, but it is a link in the chain of evidences which go far to prove that Shakespeare was, at some period, a traveller by sea.

48. tang, twang.

55. Ind, India.

56. your, used colloquially, as in *Hamlet*, iv. 3. 22, 23: "Your worm is your only emperor for diet".

58. give ground, give way.

62, 63. should he learn, should he have learnt, so as to be able to speak it.

64. recover, restore.

66. neat's-leather, cow leather used in shoes. Cf. *Julius Cæsar,* i. 1. 28, 29: "As proper men as ever trod upon neat's leather"

72. I will not take too much for him, whatever I get for him will not be too much.

75. trembling, a sign of being possessed by a devil.

76. Come on your ways. 'Ways' is probably the old gen. used adverbially. Wright compares the German 'er zog seines Weges', 'he went his ways'.

77. cat, alluding to the proverb, "good liquor will make a cat speak".

86. Amen! stop, that is enough for this mouth.

89, 90. I have no long spoon. This alludes to the custom in the Morality Plays of the *Vice,* furnished with a long wooden spoon, eating out of the same dish as the Devil. Cf. *Comedy of Errors,* iv. 3. 64: "Marry, he must have a long spoon that must eat with the devil".

96. very Trinculo, the real Trinculo.

103, 104. is not constant, is unsettled.

105. an if. See note on ii. 1. 172.

115. Stephano does not take any notice of Caliban's interruption, but again presses Trinculo to swear upon the bottle how he escaped.

126. when time was, once upon a time.

133. Well drawn, a good draught.

142. I could find it in my heart, I feel inclined.

155. pig-nuts: the tuber or root-stock of the plant known as the *Bunium flexuosum.* It is round and brown, white inside, and pleasant to the taste. It cannot be pulled up by force, but needs to be "dug" for.

159. scamels. The word may either mean (1) 'limpets', a diminutive of *scam,* shell-fish, derived from the Norse *skama* or shell; or (2) some kind of rock-breeding bird. Stevenson, in his *Birds of Norfolk,* says that the female bar-tailed Godwit is called a *scamell* by the gunners of Blakeney. But this bird is not a rock-breeder, and therefore either Caliban's description is not accurate, or the word in Shakespeare's time must have had a wider application. Of the numerous conjectural readings the most plausible is *sea-mells* or sea-malls (Theobald, Steevens, Malone, Harting), *i.e.* 'sea-gulls'. Young sea-gulls were formerly considered great delicacies, and were captured before they could fly.

162. inherit, take possession.

169. trencher. The Ff. read *trenchering.* Pope's emendation has been usually accepted, though Grant White thinks that Caliban, being drunk, would naturally sing "trenchering" after "firing" and "requiring".

Act III.—Scene I.

This scene strikes more clearly than any other the chief key-note of the play—that true freedom consists in service. Ferdinand and Miranda are both eager to undertake the lowest drudgery for the other's sake, and thus prove that their love, though so sudden, is of the type that will endure (see Introduction, §§ 25, 26). Moulton holds that in the introduction of this episode of "love at first sight" Shakespeare intends "to give increased reality to the story" by including one of the "elements of common life that have kinship with enchantment" (p. 239). But this, though he works it out very ingeniously, is extremely doubtful. Instances of love at first sight are far too common in the Shakespearian drama for special significance to be attached to the episode in *The Tempest*. Shakespeare even quotes with approval, *As You Like It* (iii. 5. 82), Marlowe's line:

"Who ever loved, that loved not at first sight?"

1. There be some sports are painful. For the omission of the relative cf. Abbott, § 244, and for the use of *be* cf. Abbott, § 300.

1, 2. and their labour Delight in them sets off. (1) *Labour* may be nominative to *sets off*, and *delight* accusative, in which case *sets off* means 'heightens by contrast'. This is the sense in which "sets off" is most frequently used by Shakespeare, and this rendering best suits the use of *and*. (2) *Delight* may be the nominative and *labour* the accusative. In favour of this is the more natural sequence of acc. nom. verb, instead of nom. acc. verb. In this case *sets off* means 'is a set off against', 'removes'.

3, 4. most poor matters Point to rich ends, very mean transactions or operations have rich issues in view.

5. heavy, burdensome.

6. quickens, gives life to.

11. sore injunction, an injunction laid upon me with a sore penalty attached.

13. I forget, *i.e.* to go on with my work.

15. Most busy lest, when I do it. These words form one of the most difficult problems in Shakespearian textual criticism. The different emendations and interpretations of the passage since the time of Pope occupy twelve pages of Furness' *Variorum* edition. As it stands it cannot be construed. Of the emendations suggested the following are the most important: (1) *Most busy, least when I do it.* This is the reading of the later Ff. except that they put the comma after 'least'. The passage may then be paraphrased, 'I forget to go on with my work, but these sweet thoughts about my mistress do, as a matter of fact, give fresh alacrity to my labours, and so I am really most engaged on my task, when I am least occupied with it'. With this interpretation we must look on the natural order of "least when" as reversed, and "it" as referring to 'the work' understood from "my labours" in the previous line. (2) *Most busiest* (or possibly *busil'est* for *busilyest*) *when I do it.* In this case "it" refers to "forget", and we interpret, 'I am most busy (for my mind is so occupied with thoughts) just when I am forgetting my work, and so seem idle'. (3) Spedding conjectures, *most busiest, when idlest*, which Wright regards as on the whole the best suggestion yet made. (4) *Most busiless when I do it*, 'least busy when engaged in the work, because the thought of my mistress makes the task seem trivial. This is, however, most unlikely, for *busiless* is found nowhere else, and is a word of more than questionable formation.

31. worm, used in the sense of 'creature' as a term of commiseration.

32. visitation: suggested by "infected" in the previous line, both words being used of the plague.

37. broke, for 'broken'. Cf. Abbott, § 343.

38. the top of admiration, that which admiration cannot go beyond.

46. put it to the foil, foiled, defeated.

52. features: used in E.E. of the whole bodily shape, not, as now, merely of the face. Cf. *Richard III.*, i. 1. 19, where the hunchback king complains that he is "Cheated of feature by dissembling nature".

53. skill-less of, ignorant of.

62. wooden slavery, bondage of bearing logs.

than to suffer. For the construction cf. Abbott, § 350: "*To* is often omitted in the former of two clauses and inserted in the latter, particularly when the finite principal verb is an auxiliary or like an auxiliary".

70. hollowly, insincerely.

invert, change, pervert.

71. What: used for the indefinite pronoun 'any' or 'anything'. Cf. Abbott, § 255.

78. and much less take, and much less dare take.

79. die to want, die through wanting. Cf. Abbott, § 356.

80. it relates to nothing expressed by Miranda, but to what her characteristic delicacy shrinks from naming—love.

81-86. "Miranda speaks with the sacred candour from which spring the nobler manners of a world more real and glad than the world of convention and proprieties and pruderies" (Dowden). A similar instance of this "sacred candour" is Elaine's declaration of love to Lancelot, in *The Idylls of the King.*

84. fellow, companion.

94. book, the magician's conjuring-book. The last cry of Marlowe's Faustus, as the devils come to drag him to hell, is, "I'll burn my books".

Scene 2.

In this scene we see that the conspiracy against Prospero, so enthusiastically started, is not prospering. Quarrels between Trinculo and Caliban are already disturbing the unity of the "triple alliance", and Ariel's unseen interference provokes a downright hand-to-hand encounter between Stephano and "lieutenant" Trinculo. But peace is patched up for a time, and Stephano inspirits the company with his song, which Dowden has jestingly named "the *Marseillaise* of the enchanted island".

2. bear up: a nautical phrase, meaning to "put the helm up, and keep a vessel off her course".

2, 3. Servant-monster. For Ben Jonson's mockery of this phrase cf. Introduction, § 7.

4. the folly of this island: apparently a toast which Trinculo proposes to Caliban to drink.

6. brained like us, having brains like ours.

8. set in thy head, having a fixed look through drinking. In the next line Trinculo interprets the words literally.

14. standard, standard-bearer.

15. he's no standard, he's too drunk to stand.

23, 24. in case to justle, in the humour for justling.

24. deboshed, debauched.

52. this thing, Trinculo.

dare not, would not dare under any circumstances; stronger than 'dares'.

64. quick freshes, the living springs of fresh water.

67. make a stock-fish of thee, beat thee as a stock-fish (dried cod) is beaten before it is boiled.

85. paunch him, run him through the paunch or belly.

88. nor hath not. For the double negative cf. Abbott, § 406.

90. but, only.

91. utensils, apparently accented on the first syllable.

92. 'With which he will deck his house, when he has it.' The clause 'which he'll deck his house withal' is interrupted by the change to 'when he has a house'

93. that, that which.

to consider, to be considered. Cf. Abbott, § 405.

96. she, for 'her'. Cf. Abbott, § 211.

98. Is it so brave a lass? For this use of *it* cf. i. 2. 310.

112. but while-ere, only a short time since.

113. do reason, do what is reasonable.

117. Thought is free. This was a proverbial expression; cf. *Twelfth Night*, i. 3. 73: "Now, sir, 'thought is free'". Furness refers to Skelton's *Phyllyp Sparowe*, l. 1201: "Thought is franke and fre"; and Wright quotes an instance of the phrase from Lyly's *Euphues.*

120, 121. the picture of Nobody. We cannot identify the exact picture alluded to; it may have been the print of *Nobody*, depicted as a man, with merely head, arms, and legs, which is prefixed to the anonymous comedy, *Nobody is Somebody*, printed before 1600; or it may have been the engraving on an old ballad, *The Well-spoken Nobody*, which represents a ragged man surrounded by broken household utensils, and bearing the motto, "Nobody is my name that beareth everybodyes blame".

136. that, so that.

141. by and by, may here, like 'presently' in E.E., mean 'immediately', or it may = 'shortly' as in *1 Henry IV.*, v. 4. 109: "Imbowelled will I see thee by-and-by".

146. Wilt come? These words have been transferred by some critics to Stephano. But they are probably addressed by Trinculo to Caliban, who, vexed at his companions for running after the music instead of hurrying to Prospero's cell, may have lingered behind.

Scene 3.

Antonio and Sebastian are still intent on carrying out the fell design against Alonso in which they have been once foiled, but they are now to have their misdeeds brought home to them with appalling suddenness. They find themselves bidden to a mysterious banquet, only for it to vanish in thunder and lightning, whence Ariel in harpy-form warns them of their doom. "The whole past stands out before them as no more than the story of one foul deed and its avenging; the very sea which they had made the innocent accomplice of their crime has bided his time to requite them, and the shores, yea, every creature, are incensed against them. The future looms before them as lingering perdition stretching beyond death....All space and time seems to have resolved itself into a trap of fate for them; and there is but one small avenue of escape hinted at in 'heart-sorrow and a clear life ensuing'" (Moulton). Alonso is moved to repentance by the strange apparition, but Antonio and Sebastian are inspired to fresh fury for the time.

1. By 'r lakin, by our ladykin, or little lady, *i.e.* by the Virgin.

3. forth-rights and meanders, straight paths and tortuous windings.

8. for my flatterer, to flatter me.

11. he's so out of hope, there's no hope of his being still alive.

14. throughly, thoroughly.

15. oppress'd, overcome.

Stage-direction, *Above*. The Ff. read *on the top*, "meaning, perhaps, in some machine let down with ropes from the ceiling, or possibly only in the balcony at the back of the stage".

21. A living drollery. A *drollery*, in Shakespeare's time, meant 'a puppet-show'. A living drollery is a show in which the figures are not wooden dolls, but living persons.

22-24. Pliny, to whom we owe our original information about the *Phœnix*, confesses ignorance as to "whether it be a tale or no that there is never but one of them in all the world, and the same not commonly seen". Pliny describes the bird 'by report' as being "as big as an Ægle; for colour, as yellow and bright as gold (namely, all about the necke); the rest of the bodie a deep red purple; the taile azure blew". For the further legend, that there is only *one* tree in Arabia on which the Phœnix builds, cf. *The Phœnix and the Turtle*:

> "Let the bird of loudest lay,
> On the sole Arabian tree,
> Herald sad and trumpet be".

25. what does else want credit, whatever likewise is incredible.

31, 32. Who...Their manners are. We should expect 'who are more gentle in their manners', but the construction is irregular. Cf. *Merchant of Venice*, iv. 1. 134, 135:

> "a wolf, who, hang'd for human slaughter,
> Even from the gallows did his fell soul fleet".

36, 37. muse Such shapes. If we adopt the punctuation of the Ff., which puts no stop after *muse*, we must treat the word as a transitive verb governing *such shapes*, and meaning 'wonder at'. This construction, however, is not used elsewhere by Shakespeare, and Keightley may therefore have been right in punctuating as follows:

> "I cannot too much muse.
> Such shapes, such gesture and such sound, expressing
> . . . . . a kind
> Of excellent dumb discourse!"

39. Praise in departing. A proverbial phrase, meaning 'do not praise till the entertainment is over'. A play of Stephen Gosson's was called *Praise at Parting*.

45, 46. This has been generally understood to refer to *goitre*, a disease common in mountainous districts. But Furness doubts whether so wide-spread and well-known a disease could be spoken of as an incredible traveller's tale, and also whether the word 'wallet' could be used of a mere excrescence of flesh. He believes that some such legend is alluded to as is related concerning The Satyrs in a collection of tales made by Gesner: "They cary their meat vnder their chin as in a storehouse, and from thence being hungry they take it forth to eate".

46, 47. Cf. *Othello*, i. 3. 144, 145:

> "The Anthropophagi and men whose heads
> Do grow beneath their shoulders".

This may have been suggested by Raleigh's statement in his *Discovery of Guiana* (1598): "On that branch which is called *Caora* are a nation of people, whose heads appear not above their shoulders....They are reported to have eyes in their shoulders, and their mouths in the middle of their breasts".

48. Each putter-out of five for one. An elliptical phrase, meaning 'each putter out of a principal for a return of five pounds on each pound left in deposit'. Travellers in the Elizabethan age, and afterwards, used at the beginning of a journey to deposit a sum with a financial agent, who kept the money if they died on the journey, and paid them five pounds for every one if they returned safely. This is made evident by a passage in Ben Jonson's *Every Man out of his Humour*, ii. 1, where Puntarvalo says, "I do intend ...to travel...and I am determined to put forth some five thousand pound to be paid me, five for one, upon the return of myself, my wife, and my dog from the Turk's court in Constantinople. If all or either of us miscarry in the journey, 'tis gone; if we be successful, why, there will be five and twenty thousand pound to entertain time withal."

53–56. whom ... you. On the supplementary pronoun cf. Abbott, § 249.

54. to instrument. Cf. note on ii. 1. 70.

55, 56. The natural order of the words would be: '(destiny) hath caused the never-surfeited sea to belch you up'.

60. proper selves, their own selves.

fellows. Cf. note on iii. 1. 84.

62. Of whom, for the use of *whom* with a neuter antecedent cf. Abbott, § 264.

64. still-closing, constantly closing over the wounds made in them.

65. dowle, equivalent to 'down'. Steevens quotes from a small book, *Humane Industry, or a History of most Manual Arts*, 1661, the following illustrative passages: "The wool-bearing trees in Æthiopia, which Virgil speaks of...are not such trees as have a certain wool or *dowl* upon the outside of them, as the small cotton;

but short trees that bear a ball upon the top, pregnant with wool. There is a certain shell-fish in the sea, called Pinna, that bears a mossy *dowl* or wool, whereof cloth was spun and made". A writer in *Notes and Queries*, 1859, mentions that in Gloucestershire the plumage of young goslings, before they have feathers, is called *dowle*.

66. like, similarly.

67. massy, massive.

71. requit. Cf. note on i. 2. 31.

77, 78. worse than any death Can be at once, worse than any instantaneous death can be.

79. whose. The antecedent is *powers* in l. 73.

80. falls should be plural after 'wraths which', but is attracted into the singular by the intervening substantive 'isle'. Cf. Abbott, § 412.

82. clear, innocent, pure.

83–86. 'You have omitted no part of my instructions as to what you were to say, and similarly my subordinate agents have carried out with lifelike exactitude and rare attention their separate functions'.

92. whom they suppose is drowned. A confusion of two constructions, 'whom they suppose to be drowned' and 'who, they suppose, is drowned'. Cf. Abbott, § 410.

93. mine. For the use of *mine* as a pronominal adjective *before* its noun cf. Abbott, § 238.

96. it, my crime against Prospero. Alonso alludes in this indefinite way to his former wickedness, as Miranda, in iii. 1. 80, to her love.

99. did bass my trespass, proclaimed my guilt in its deep bass roar.

102. But one fiend at a time, let there be but one fiend at a time.

Act IV.—Scene I.

This scene is occupied principally by the elaborate masque, the "vanity" of his "art", which Prospero has performed in honour of Ferdinand and Miranda. The length of this masque, and the prominence given to it in the very centre of the play, whose action it delays at a critical juncture, leave no doubt that *The Tempest*, like *A Midsummer-Night's Dream*, was intended to celebrate the wedding of some high-born personages. In the opinion of some critics the wedding was that of the Elector Palatine and the Princess Elizabeth (see Introduction, § 7). The underlying conception of the masque is the fruitfulness of nature culminating in the fruitfulness of a prosperous wedlock. Thus "the suggestions of nature . . . scattered broadcast through every scene are gathered to a climax" in this masque, "which has for its function to pour forth a prodigal accumulation of nature-wealth. In form it is a meeting of mythical deities; but the language presents them as embodiments of the different elements of landscape" (Moulton). The second part of the scene shows the ignominious collapse of the conspiracy against Prospero, though Caliban proves his superiority to his companions by remaining firm to the original aim of the plot, while they let themselves be turned aside by the prospect of some paltry plunder.

3. **third.** This is the Ff. reading, and there is no sufficient reason for changing it. Prospero probably only uses the word vaguely to express that Miranda forms a main portion of his very being. Furness, somewhat strangely, supports Capell's view that the phrase has a more definite meaning, the three thirds of Prospero's life being his realm, his daughter, and himself. It has been suggested that *third* is a variant spelling of *thrid* or *thread*, and Hawkins quotes from the comedy of *Mucedorus* (1619): "To cut in twaine the twisted *third* of life". But the reading is doubtful. Many editors have adopted the reading *thrid*, which means a 'fibre', and would signify here 'one of my heart-strings'.

4. **who.** Cf. note on i. 2. 231.

7. **strangely,** rarely, wonderfully.

9. **boast her off**: the reading of the later Ff., and of practically all editors. The phrase *boast off* is otherwise unknown in Shakespeare's writings, and it is just possible, as Furness suggests, that the reading of F 1, "boast her of", is merely a transposition for 'boast of her'. But the accepted reading is far the most expressive of the two.

16. **sanctimonious,** here used in the sense of 'holy'.

18. **aspersion,** in the literal sense of 'sprinkling' as of 'dew'.

21. **weeds**: instead of the flowers with which the bridal bed was strewn.

22, 23. **take heed, As Hymen's lamps shall light you**: take heed, and only act as Hymen's lamps by their light shall give you authority to do. Another explanation, involving an unusual but not unprecedented use of *as* = 'so that', is 'do nothing to prevent Hymen's lamps lighting you'. But Ferdinand in his reply does not seem to anticipate that, in any case, Prospero would prevent his marriage. Elze is probably right in his suggestion that *lamps* is a misprint for *lamp*, the *s* intruding into the text by anticipation of the initial *s* in *shall*. Hymen, the god of marriage, has only one lamp, or "torch", as it is called in l. 97.

26. **opportune**: the accent is on the second syllable.

suggestion: cf. note on ii. 1. 278.

27. **genius.** A comparison of the chief passages in which the word *genius* is used by Shakespeare shows that it is employed in the sense of a 'spirit' conceived of as resident within a man, and constituting, in the strict sense, his personality. Cf. *Julius Cæsar*, ii. 1. 63–67:

> "Between the acting of a dreadful thing
> And the first motion, all the interim is
> Like a phantasma or a hideous dream.
> The Genius and the mortal instruments
> Are then in council".

i.e. the spirit and the bodily powers with which it works are holding debate together. Cf. also *Macbeth*, iii. 1. 55–57:

> "under him
> My Genius is rebuked; as, it is said,
> Mark Antony's was by Cæsar".

This passage is explained by *Antony and Cleopatra*, ii. 3. 18–22:

> "Therefore, O Antony, stay not by his side:
> Thy demon, that's thy spirit which keeps thee, is
> Noble, courageous, high, unmatchable,
> Where Cæsar's is not; but near him, thy angel
> Becomes a fear, as being o'erpowered".

Here we see that the "spirit" or "genius" is indifferently spoken of as "demon" or "angel". The spirit that has taken lodging in human abode may be good or evil (cf. i. 2. 458, 459), and a variation of the idea represents two spirits or "genii" conflicting for the empire over the man. Hence the reference here to "Our *worser* genius", with which we may compare Sonnet cxliv.:

> "Two loves I have of comfort and despair,
> Which like two spirits do suggest me still.
> The better angel is a man right fair,
> The worser spirit a woman colour'd ill".

can, can make.

30. **Phœbus' steeds**, a reference to the myth that the sun-god drove round the world in a four-horsed car.

founder'd, crippled and unable to move. "Foundering cometh when a horse is heated and taketh theron a suddaine cold which striketh downe into his legs, and taking away the vse and feeling thereof."—Topsell, *The History of Foure-footed Beasts* (1608).

31. **spoke**, spoken. Cf. Abbott, § 343.

33. **What;** used as a mode of calling.

37. **rabble;** used of the company of "meaner ministers", but without any contemptuous sense.

41. **vanity**, illusion.

42. **Presently**, immediately, which is its usual sense in E.E.

54. good night your vow, farewell to your vow.

56. liver: supposed to be the seat of passion.

57. corollary, a supernumerary (see Glossary). Prospero bids Ariel bring more spirits than are necessary rather than have one too few.

60–138. The merits of this masque have been very variously estimated. Capell speaks of it as written "against the grain seemingly, being weak throughout, faulty in rhymes, and faulty in its mythology; matters not within the province of Ceres, such as 'sheep' and 'vines', are attributed to her". Hartley Coleridge asserts that "there is not much either of melody or meaning in this masque. Prospero, when his spell enforced attendance of the spirits, should have furnished them with smoother couplets and sager discourse." The German critic Hense, on the other hand, declares that "the masque of the goddesses in *The Tempest* is pre-eminent for its lyric beauty". This is an extravagantly favourable verdict, for Iris' opening speech, with its detailed catalogue of country products and scenes, is undeniably prosaic. But the lines describing Venus and her son (87–101) contain some charming images, and are entirely worthy of Shakespeare's pen. In any case it is unwarrantable to assign the masque to another hand, as some critics have done, because the couplets lack smoothness. On the contrary, this is an argument for its genuineness. The rhyming passages in Shakespeare's later plays are few, but where they occur, they show, as here, the same characteristics as mark his blank verse of the same period. We have 'run-on' instead of 'end-stopt' lines, and more care for energy and incisiveness of expression than for sweetness of melody.

61. vetches: spelt "fetches" in the Ff. This is still the common provincial pronunciation of the word.

63. stover "is the term now applied to the coarser hay made of clover and artificial grasses, which is kept for the winter feed of cattle. . . . In the sixteenth century the word was apparently used to denote any kind of winter fodder except grass hay. (Illustrations follow from Tusser and Drayton.) The word is derived from the Old French, *estavoir, estovoir, estouvier,* or *estouvoir,* which denotes, according to Roquefort (*Glossaire de la langue Romane*), 'provision de tout ce qui est nécessaire'" (Wright).

64. banks, either 'river-banks', or, more probably, 'mounds' between the 'flat meads', which would naturally be in the care of Ceres.

pioned and twilled. The explanations of these obscure terms fall into two main groups. (1) They refer to the *flowers* or *grasses* growing on the banks. *Pioned* is interpreted as being the same word as *peonied, i.e.* covered with peonies. The peony is not suited to make "chaste crowns" for nymphs, but T. S. Baynes asserted on the authority of "a clergyman long resident in the north of Warwick" that the marsh-marigold was provincially known as the peony. Doubt has, however, been thrown on the correctness of this assertion. *Twilled* was declared by Baynes to refer to the sedges on a river's bank, *twills* being a provincial word for reeds. But though *twills* is given by Ray as equivalent to 'quills' or 'reeds' for winding yarn, there is no evidence of its being used for 'reeds' in the sense of a plant. Another interpretation of *twilled brims* is that it means banks fringed with thickly-matted grass, resembling *twilled* cloth in which the cords appear closely twisted together. (2) The words more probably do not refer to flowers at all, for the banks seem to be spoken of as 'pioned and twilled' *before* April "betrims" them. In this case some agricultural operations are alluded to. *Pioning* is used by Spenser in the sense of "digging", *Faerie Queene*, ii. 10:

> "with painful pyonings
> From sea to sea he heaped a mighty mound".

Twilled may be connected with the French *touiller*, to begrime or besmear, and the passage, according to Henley, refers to "the repairing of the brims of banks, which have given way, by opening the trenches from whence the banks themselves were at first raised, and facing them up afresh with the mire those trenches contain".

66. broom-groves. The phrase presents a difficulty because "grove" does not seem applicable to a shrub like "broom". But we may compare the place-name, Bromsgrove. Hanmer conjectured "brown".

67. dismisséd bachelor, rejected suitor.

68. lass-lorn, forsaken of his mistress.

pole-clipt vineyard, the vineyard in which the vines are twined about the poles. *Clip* means 'to twine round' or 'embrace', and the passive form of the participle is here used actively.

74. peacocks, the birds that draw the chariot of Juno.

85. freely, liberally.

estate, bestow.

89. dusky Dis: Pluto, who carried off Ceres' daughter, Proserpina.

93. Paphos: a town in Cyprus, which contained a celebrated temple of Venus.

99. waspish-headed, irritable.

100. sparrows. The sparrow was sacred to Venus; hence its association with the goddess and with Cupid in literature. Chaucer in *The Parlement of Foules* calls the sparrow 'Venus' son'. In Lyly's song 'Cupid and my Campaspe', the god of love

> ". . . stakes his quiver, bow and arrows,
> His mother's doves and team of sparrows".

110. **plenty,** plentiful.

114, 115. Compare with these lines Spenser's *Faerie Queene*, iii. 6. 42:

> "There is continuall spring, and harvest there
> Continuall, both meeting at one time".

119, 120. **bold To think,** so bold as to think.

121. **confines,** limits to which they are confined.

123. **wonder'd,** able to perform wonders. Cf. Abbott, § 294.

and a wise. Rowe conjectured 'wife', which was adopted by Pope. But Ferdinand is for the time absorbed in wonder at Prospero's magic power; moreover, 'wife' without any epithet sounds bald after the enthusiastic outburst that precedes.

124. **Sweet, now.** These words would seem more naturally addressed to Miranda, and it has been suggested that they are a continuation of Ferdinand's speech, which is interrupted by Prospero's "silence!" But probably no change is necessary; Shakespeare in the *Sonnets* addresses his young friend "Will" as "sweet love".

126. **to do,** to be done. Cf. Abbott, § 405.

128. **windring:** the reading of the Ff. Probably 'winding' or 'wand'ring' is correct.

130. **crisp,** curled with the ripple of the water.

138. **footing,** dancing.

142. **avoid,** begone.

144. **works him strongly,** affects him powerfully.

145. **distemper'd,** discomposed.

146. **sort,** manner.

150–156. On the likeness between these lines and a passage from Stirling's *Tragedy of Darius* cf. Introduction, § 3.

157. **a rack.** The phrase, *the rack*, derived from O.E. *réc*, smoke (cf. German *rauch*, smoke), is used of the filmy upper clouds. Cf. Bacon, *Sylva Sylvarum*: "The winds in the upper region (which move the clouds above, which we call the rack, and are not perceived below) pass without noise". Cf., too, *Antony and Cleopatra*, iv. 14. 9, 10:

> "even with a thought
> The rack dislimns".

A rack, however, to signify a single, small cloud, has not been found, though the plural, "the rackes", occurs in a poem of 1608, and Lydgate uses the phrase "every rak". The use of the word here seems to be suggested by the unsubstantial pageant of the marriage masque which has just faded. In Ben Jonson's *Hymenaei*, a marriage masque introducing Juno and Iris, the upper part of the scene is described as being "all of clouds, and made artificially to swell and ride like the rack". Evidently similar machinery was used here, and the poet applies the word *rack* to clouds as a constituent part of the machinery of the pageant. "Mark" (as one critic has interpreted it), "says Prospero, the little pageant that has just passed before your eyes, and is now vanished into thin air. It is thus that the great Pageant of the world shall itself finally be no more; not even the minutest portion of this vast machinery shall escape the general destruction—not a *rack*, not an atom shall remain". Malone and Dyce, on account of the difficulty involved in *a rack*, conjectured that *rack* was a misspelling of *wrack* or *wreck*, and that Prospero asserts that not only will the cloud-capped towers, &c., dissolve, but that their very wrecks or ruins will vanish from human sight. This interpretation, however, is unconvincing.

157. on, of.

158. rounded, either 'surrounded' or 'finished off with', 'completed'.

163. beating, agitated.

164. with a thought, as quick as thought.

I thank thee, Ariel, *i.e.* for the masque so skilfully managed.

165. cleave to, follow closely.

166. meet with, counteract, check.

167. presented, represented.

177. Advanced their eyelids. Cf. note on i. 2. 407.

178. As, as if. Cf. Abbott, § 107.

180. goss, gorse.

182. filthy-mantled, covered with a filthy scum. Cf. *King Lear*, iii. 4. 138, 139: "drinks the green mantle of the standing pool".

184. feet. This, the reading of the Ff., does not give a very satisfactory sense, but nothing is gained by the proposed emendations of 'feat' or 'fear'. The passage may mean that the filth at the bottom of the pool was stirred up by their dancing, and rose, smelling vilely, above their feet.

189. Nurture, training.

190. taken, bestowed.

192. cankers, grows corrupt. With the passage we may compare Essex' ungallant speech about Queen Elizabeth: "that she grew old and canker'd, and that her mind was become as crooked as her carcase".

193. Even to roaring, till they roar.

line may be explained in two ways—(1) *lime tree*, in which case Prospero refers to a tree of "the line-grove which weather-fends" his cell, cf. v. 1. 10, where many editors have altered the Ff. reading to '*lime*-grove'; but *line* was the more usual form of the word. (2)

Clothes-line, the alternative interpretation, is, *à priori,* less probable, for it is incongruous to suppose that such an appliance of civilization should be hanging outside of Prospero's cell. Yet it must be allowed that this interpretation gives more point to Stephano's jests in lines 236–239. The words "now is the jerkin under the line" are more applicable in the case of a cord than of a tree, and the joke about the jerkin losing its hair and proving 'a bald jerkin' seems to refer to the fact that clothes-lines in Shakespeare's time were usually made of hair.

197. played the Jack. Either 'played Jack with the lantern', and so beguiled us into the mire; or 'played the knave or rogue'. Cf. *Much Ado about Nothing,* i. 1. 185–187: "do you play the flouting Jack, to tell us Cupid is a good harefinder?"

203. hoodwink, blindfold; hence here 'cover', 'put out of sight'.

215. I, for 'me'. Cf. Abbott, § 209.

218, 219. The allusion is to the ballad containing the stanza:

> "King Stephen was a worthy peere,
>   His breeches cost him but a crowne,
> He held them sixpence all too deere;
>   Therefore he called the taylor Lowne".

227. Let's alone. This is the reading of the Ff., and, if correct, has the sense of 'let's along'. Staunton quotes from Beaumont and Fletcher's *Loyal Subject,* iii. 5, a passage where *alone* is used in the sense of 'along', and where it cannot be a misprint, as it rhymes with 'gone'. A conjectural reading is 'Let it alone', repeating the words in l. 220.

231–233. These words contain a complex series of puns (1) *Now is the jerkin under the line* is probably a reference to the custom at tennis of staking the wager under the line, so as to be taken by the winner. Thus, as Stephano advances towards the jerkin, he cries that it *now* hangs up ready for a claimant; then as he utters the second *now* he pulls the garment off the line and makes the joke about its losing its hair, explained in the note on l. 193. (2) *Under the line* is also a slang phrase for 'hanging by the neck', as is shown by Staunton's quotation from *An Elegy upon Edward Dun, Esq., the Citie's Common Hangman, who Dyed Naturally in his Bed,* 1663:

> "It was (oh, Death!) an unjust thing,
>   Thou should'st deny him his own swing;
> Sure, sure, thou hadst some great designe,
>   Or else thou 'adst took him *under-line*".

(3) There may be a further reference to the nautical phrase *under the line,* and the fevers often contracted there, which cause loss of hair.

234. by line and level, according to rule, methodically; a metaphor taken from carpentry. The phrase is merely introduced as another pun upon 'line'.

238. pass of pate, sally of wit.

240. lime, bird-lime. As the punning upon 'line' is still being continued, 'line' and 'lime' must evidently have been convertible forms in this, as in other senses of the word.

243. barnacles, geese which were supposed to breed out of certain shell-fish which grew upon trees.

244. foreheads villanous low. A low forehead was counted a deformity in Shakespeare's time.

255. aged cramps. Cf. note on i. 2. 369.

258. Lie. Rowe's correction for the Ff. reading *lies*, which may, however, be supported on the analogy of i. 1. 15.

Act V.—Scene I.

Prospero, having all his enemies at his mercy, makes use of his magic power for the last time, before he lays it aside for ever. He releases them from the trance into which they have been plunged, and extends to them degrees of pardon (cf. Introduction, § 24), while Gonzalo is embraced with loving words. Thereupon follow universal reunion and restoration. Ferdinand, with his newly-won bride, is given back to his father's arms. The Master and the Boatswain rejoin their fellow-voyagers and report that the ship, which had been given up for lost, is safe in 'all her trim'. Caliban and his allies are driven in to be claimed by their respective masters, and to be forgiven on condition of penitence, and surrender of stolen goods. Ariel is restored to his home, the air; and finally Prospero strains his eyes across seas towards his Milan, and beyond that, towards his grave.

2. crack not. This probably refers to the magic bonds which Prospero weaves round his victims. Thus he afterwards declares (line 31) "my charms I'll break".

3. Goes upright with his carriage, marches on erect, not bending under his load.

10. line-grove. Cf. note on iv. 1. 193.

weather-fends, protects from the weather.

11. till your release, till released by you.

15. Him, for 'he'. Cf. Abbott, § 208.

17. strongly works 'em. Cf. iv. 1. 144.

21. a touch, a power of sensibility.

23, 24. relish all as sharply, Passion as they. If we keep this punctuation of F 1 and F 2, *passion* is a verb (cf. *Venus and Adonis*, 1059: "Dumbly she passions"; and *Two Gentlemen of Verona*, iv. 4. 172: "'t was Ariadne passioning"). The words then mean 'feel joy just as keenly, and am as much moved with sorrow as they'. F 3 and F 4 omit the comma after 'sharply', thus treating 'passion' as a noun governed by 'relish'.

33–50. This passage has so remarkable a likeness in its phraseology to Medea's incantation in Golding's translation of Ovid's *Metamorphoses*, that it must have been partly modelled on it. Wright quotes the following passage from the edition of 1603:

"Ye Ayres and Windes: ye Elues of Hilles, of Brookes, of Woods alone,
Of standing Lakes, and of the Night approche ye euerychone;
Through helpe of whom (the crooked bankes much wondring at the thing)
I have compelled streames to run cleane backward to their spring.
By charmes I make the calme seas rough, and make the rough seas playne,
And couer all the Skie with clouds and chase them thence againe;
By charmes I raise and lay the windes, and burst the Vipers iaw,
And from the bowels of the earth both stones and trees do draw.
Whole woods and Forrests I remoue: I make the Mountaines shake,
And euen the earth it selfe to grone and fearefully to quake;
I call up dead men from their graues, and thee, O lightsome Moone,
I darken oft, though beaten brasse abate thy peril soone;
Our sorceries dimmes the Morning faire, and darkes the Sun at Noone."

37. green sour ringlets: the circles of a deeper green than the surrounding grass, and bitterer in taste, which are found in meadows, and which were popularly supposed to be caused by the dancing of fairies.

41. Weak masters, weak adepts in magical powers.

43. azured, azure. Cf. Abbott, § 294.

47. spurs, the roots which project.

51. required, asked for.

59. unsettled fancy, distorted imagination.

60. boil'd. The Ff. read *boile*. For the use of the word in this connection cf. *Winter's Tale*, iii. 3. 64, 65: "Would any but these boiled brains of nineteen and two-and-twenty hunt this weather?"

63. sociable to, in sympathy with.
    show, appearance.

64. Fall. Cf. ii. 1. 286, note.
    fellowly, companionable.

67. **ignorant**, producing ignorance.

71. **Home**, thoroughly. Cf. *Measure for Measure*, iv. 3. 148: "Accuse him home and home".

76. **remorse**, pity.

81. **reasonable shore**, the shore of reason.

85. **discase me**, strip off my disguise.

86. **Milan**, Duke of Milan. Cf. i. 2. 109.

90. **when owls do cry**, *i.e.* at night.

92. **summer**, changed by Theobald into 'sunset', on the ground that bats do not migrate with the close of summer. But Shakespeare is here dealing with fairy-lore, not with natural history, and the idea of spirits flying after summer is akin to that in *Midsummer-Night's Dream*, iv. 1. 101: "Trip we after the night's shade".

102. **drink the air**, an analogous expression to 'devour the way'.

103. **Or ere**. Cf. note on i. 2. 11.

112. **trifle**, phantom.
abuse, deceive.

117. **An if this be at all**, if this have any real existence.

118. **Thy dukedom I resign.** Antonio had made Milan a fief of Naples, and Alonso herewith disclaims the sovereign rights he had thus acquired.

119. **my wrongs**, the wrongs I have done.

120. **noble friend**, Gonzalo.

123, 124. **taste Some subtilties o' the isle.** *Taste* used in the sense of 'experience' probably suggested *subtilties*, which besides meaning, as here, 'deceptions', denoted devices in pastry. Wright quotes from Fabyan's account of the feast at the coronation of Katharine, queen of Henry V.: "And a sotyltye called a Pellycane sytting on his nest with the byrdes".

128. **justify**, prove.

129. **No.** This is a curiously curt answer to Sebastian's remark, which is, moreover, supposed to be an 'aside' not overheard by Prospero. A plausible emendation is *Now*, used as the opening of the address to Antonio.

139. **I am woe for 't.** I am sorry for it. Cf. Abbott, § 230.

145, 146. 'As great to me as it is recent; and to make the keen loss bearable I have much weaker means.'

154. **do so much admire**, are so much astonished.

155. **devour their reason**, refuse to believe what their reason tells them.

156. **do offices of truth**, perform their functions truthfully.

164. relation for a breakfast, a short story to be told at breakfast.

Stage-direction, *playing at chess.* This introduction of chess into the enchanted island, especially as Shakespeare nowhere else directly mentions the game, is so curious that attempts have been made to assign some special reason for it. Steevens thought that Shakespeare borrowed the idea from the romance of *Sir Huon de Bordeaux,* where the hero and heroine engage in the same pastime. Allen ingeniously conjectures that he made the Neapolitan prince and Miranda play chess, because Naples was at that time the chief centre of the game.

174. a score. Used either in the ordinary sense of 'twenty', or, more probably, in that of 'a stake'.

you should wrangle. "The usage of 'should' and 'would' in this sentence becomes like our own by a very slight change, 'for a score of kingdoms should you wrangle I would call it fair play'" (Wright).

181–184. Notice Miranda's "child-like *naïveté* of admiration" (Moulton) on first beholding a company of her fellow-creatures.

205. Was Milan thrust from Milan? Was Prospero, the Duke of Milan, thrust out of his Duchy.

208–213. In these lines Gonzalo expounds, with pregnant brevity, the principle of loss and restitution which underlies so many incidents in the play.

214. still, always.

216. is. Cf. note on i. 1. 15, 16.

218. blasphemy, for 'blasphemer'.

221. safely found, found safe.

223. but three glasses since. If we compare this with Alonso s statement in l. 186 we see that the boatswain's 'glass' is meant to be an *hour-glass.* Brinsley Nicholson, however (*New Shakspere Society's Transactions,* 1880–1882), quotes from *The Seaman's Grammar,* by Capt. John Smith (1627), the following words: "eight glasses, or foure houres, which is a watch". This shows that the seaman's glass in Shakespeare's time, as now, was one of *half-*an-hour, not a full hour. The technical mistake thus made proves, according to Nicholson, that Shakespeare never was at sea. But this is too weak a foundation to support so momentous a conclusion, especially in the face of much internal evidence all tending the other way.

224. tight, free from leaks.

230. of sleep, through sleep. Cf. Abbott, § 168.

238. Capering to eye her, dancing with joy at beholding her.

on a trice, in a moment (see Glossary).

244. **conduct,** conductor.

246. **infest,** vex.

247. **pick'd,** well-selected.

248. **single,** alone; referring either to 'you' or 'I', probably the former.

resolve you, give you an explanation.

249. **Which to you shall seem probable.** The antecedent to 'which' is Prospero's explanation, implied in "I'll resolve you".

every. The adjectives *all*, *each*, *both*, *every*, *other*, are sometimes interchanged in E.E. Cf. Abbott, § 12.

255. **odd.** Cf. note on i. 2. 223.

257, 258. **bully-monster.** With this slang use of *bully* as a jovial term of address cf. "bully Hercules" and "bully-rook" in *The Merry Wives of Windsor*.

266. **Is a plain fish.** For this description of Caliban cf. ii. 2. 24–26.

267. **badges.** Household servants, like Stephano and Trinculo, usually wore on their arms, as part of their livery, silver badges whereon the shield of their master was engraved.

269, 270. **one so strong That could control the moon.** For other examples of *so* followed by the relative *that*, cf. Abbott, § 279.

271. **deal in her command without her power,** either 'exercise her influence without being empowered to do so' or 'exercise her influence beyond or outside of her sphere'. For the latter use of 'without' Wright compares *2 Corinthians*, x. 13: "But we will not boast of things without our measure".

279. **reeling ripe,** so intoxicated as to be ready to reel. Cf. *Love's Labour's Lost*, v. 2. 274: "The king was weeping-ripe for a good word".

280. **gilded 'em,** made them drunk. There is probably a reference to the *aurum potabile*, drinkable gold, of the alchemists; or the reference may be to the effect of liquor in making the face to glow.

283, 284. **I shall not fear fly-blowing.** Trinculo, punning on the word 'pickle', makes this statement, because pickling meat preserved it from 'fly-blowing'.

289. **a strange thing as,** as strange a thing as. The first *as* in a comparison is often omitted.

298. **bestow,** stow away.

305. **accidents gone by,** events that have happened. Cf. line 250 above.

310. **retire me.** For other examples of verbs used by Shakespeare reflexively, but now intransitive, see Abbott, § 296.

THE EPILOGUE.

"In the Epilogue, which was written perhaps by Shakespeare, perhaps by someone acquainted with his thoughts, Prospero in his character of a man, no longer a potent enchanter, petitions the spectators of the theatre for two things, pardon and freedom. It would be straining matters to discover in this Epilogue profound significances. And yet in its playfulness it curiously falls in with the moral purport of the whole. Prospero, the pardoner, implores pardon. Shakespeare was aware—whether such be the significance (aside—for the writer's mind) of this Epilogue or not—that no life is ever lived which does not need to receive as well as to render forgiveness" (Dowden).

Many critics have doubted whether this Epilogue is by Shakespeare, chiefly because of what Grant White calls "the miserable and eminently un-Shakespearian rhythm". This critic especially falls foul of the sense-pauses in the middle of the line, *e.g.* 3 and 13. But as already been said in discussing the Masque (cf. iv. 1. 60, note), these run-on lines and unrhythmical pauses are just what we should expect from Shakespeare at this period, and are no argument against the authenticity of Epilogue.

10. An invitation to the audience to applaud. Noise was supposed to dissolve a spell.

16. **prayer**, probably suggested by the custom, prevalent at the time, of concluding the play by a prayer offered up for the sovereign.

18. **Mercy itself**, the merciful God.

frees, procures pardon from.

APPENDIX A

THE PREFACE AND PROLOGUE TO DRYDEN AND
DAVENANT'S *THE TEMPEST OR THE
ENCHANTED ISLAND* [1]

PREFACE

The writing of Prefaces to Plays, was probably invented by some
very ambitious Poet, who never thought he had done enough: Perhaps by some Ape of the French Eloquence, which uses to make a
business of a Letter of Gallantry, an examen of a Farce; and, in
short, a great pomp and ostentation of words on every trifle. This
is certainly the Talent of that Nation, and ought not to be invaded
by any other. They do that out of gaiety, which would be an im-
position upon us.

We may satisfie our selves with surmounting them in the Scene,
and safely leave them those trappings of writing, and flourishes of
the Pen, with which they adorn the borders of their Plays, and
which are indeed no more than good Landskips to a very indifferent
Picture. I must proceed no farther in this Argument, lest I run my
self beyond my excuse for writing this. Give me leave therefore
to tell you, Reader, that I do it not to set a value on anything I
have written in this Play, but out of gratitude to the memory of Sir
William Davenant, who did me the honour to join me with him in
the alteration of it.

It was originally *Shakespear's*: a Poet for whom he had particularly a high veneration, and whom he first taught me to admire.
The Play it self had formerly been acted with success in the *Black-
Fryers*: and our Excellent *Fletcher* had so great a value for it, that
he thought fit to make use of the same Design, not much varied, a
second time. Those who have seen his *Sea-Voyage*, may easily
discern that it was a Copy of *Shakespear's Tempest*: the Storm, the
Desart Island, and the Woman who had never seen a Man, are all
sufficient Testimonies of it. But *Fletcher* was not the only Poet
who made use of *Shakespear's* Plot: Sir *John Suckling*, a profess'd
admirer of our Author, has follow'd his footsteps in his *Goblins*; his
Regmella being an open imitation of *Shakespear's Miranda*; and
his Spirits, though counterfeit, yet are copied from *Ariel*. But Sir

[1] The play was produced November 7th, 1667. The Preface, dated December
1st, 1669, was probably written for the earliest publication in 1670.

William Davenant, as he was a Man of quick and piercing imagination, soon found that somewhat might be added to the design of *Shakespear*, of which neither *Fletcher* nor *Suckling* had ever thought: and therefore to put the last hand to it, he design'd the Counter part to *Shakespear's* Plot, namely, that of a Man who had never seen a Woman; that by this means those two Characters of Innocence and Love might the more illustrate and commend each other. This excellent Contrivance he was pleas'd to communicate to me, and to desire my assistance in it. I confess, that from the very first moment it so pleas'd me, that I never writ anything with more delight. I must likewise do him that justice to acknowledge, that my writing received daily his amendments, and that is the reason why it is not so faulty, as the rest which I have done, without the help or correction of so judicious a Friend. The Comical part of the Saylors were also of his invention and for the most part his writing, as you will easily discover by the Style. In the time I writ with him, I had the opportunity to observe somewhat more nearly of him than I had formerly done, when I had only a bare acquaintance with him: I found him then of so quick a fancy, that nothing was propos'd to him on which he could not suddenly produce a thought extremely pleasant and surprising: and those first thoughts of his, contrary to the old Latine Proverb, were not always the least happy. And as his fancy was quick, so likewise were the products of it remote and new. He borrowed not of any other; and his imaginations were such as could not easily enter into any other Man. His Corrections were sober and judicious: and he corrected his own writings much more severely than those of another Man, bestowing twice the time and labour in polishing, which he us'd in invention. It had perhaps been easie enough for me to have arrogated more to my self than was my due, in the writing of this Play, and to have pass'd by his name with silence in the Publication of it, with the same ingratitude which others have us'd to him, whose Writings he hath not only corrected, as he hath done this, but has had a greater inspection over them, and sometimes added whole Scenes together, which may as easily be distinguish'd from the rest, as true Gold from counterfeit by the weight. But besides the unworthiness of the Action which deterred me from it (there being nothing so base as to rob the dead of his reputation) I am satisfi'd I could never have receiv'd so much honour, in being thought the Author of any Poem, how excellent soever, as I shall from the joining my imperfections with the Merit and Name of *Shakespear* and Sir *William Davenant*.

PROLOGUE

As when a Tree's cut down, the secret Root
Lives under ground, and thence new branches shoot:
So, from old *Shakespear's* honour'd dust, this day
Springs up and buds a new reviving Play.

Shakespear, who (taught by none) did first impart
To *Fletcher* Wit, to labouring *Johnson* Art.
He, Monarch-like, gave those his Subjects Law,
And is that Nature which they paint and draw.
Fletcher reach'd that which on his heights did grow,
Whilst *Johnson* crept and gather'd all below.
This did his Love, and this his Mirth digest:
One imitates him most, the other best.
If they have since out-writ all other Men,
'T is with the drops which fell from Shakespear's pen.
The Storm which vanish'd on the neighb'ring shore,
Was taught by *Shakespear's* Tempest first to roar.
That Innocence and Beauty which did smile
In *Fletcher*, grew on this Enchanted Isle.
But *Shakespear's* Magick could not copy'd be,
Within that Circle none durst walk but he.
I must confess 't was bold, nor would you now
That liberty to vulgar Wits allow,
Which work by Magick supernatural things:
But Shakespear's Pow'r is Sacred as a King's.
Those Legends from old Priesthood were receiv'd,
And he then writ, as People then believ'd.
But, if for *Shakespear* we your grace implore,
We for our Theatre shall want it more:
Who by our dearth of Youths are forc'd t'employ
One of our Women to present a Boy.
And that's a transformation, you will say,
Exceeding all the Magick in the Play.

APPENDIX B

MRS. F. A. KEMBLE'S ALLEGORICAL INTERPRETA- TION OF *THE TEMPEST*

Many critics of *The Tempest* have endeavoured to interpret it allegorically. Thus Lowell indentifies Prospero with the Imagination, Ariel with the Fancy, Caliban with the brute understanding, Miranda with Abstract Womanhood, and Fer- dinand with Youth. Emile Montégut and Dowden (the former in all seriousness, the latter in a playful exercise of fancy) have traced in the play an allegory of the poet's dra- matic career (See the *Revue des Deux Mondes*, 1865, and Dowden's *Shakspere, His Mind and Art*, pp. 425–427). Less well known is Mrs. F. A. Kemble's interpretation, contained in a MS. note in a copy of Hanmer's edition, and printed by Furness.

"*The Tempest* is my favourite of Shakespeare's dramas. . . . Chiefly I delight in this play, because of the image it presents to my mind of the glorious supremacy of the righteous human soul over all things by which it is surrounded. Prospero is to me the representative of wise and virtuous manhood in its true relation to the combined elements of existence, the physical powers of the external world, and the varieties of character with which it comes into voluntary, accidental, or enforced contact.—Of the wonderful chain of being, of which Caliban is the densest and Ariel the most ethereal extreme, Prospero is the middle link. He—the wise and good man—is the ruling power, to whom the whole series is subject. First, and lowest in the scale, comes the gross and uncouth but powerful savage, who represents both the more ponderous and unwieldy natural elements (as the earth and water), which the wise magician by his knowledge compels to his service; and the brutal and animal propensities of the nature of man which he, the type of its noblest development, holds in lordly subjugation.—Next follow the drunken, ribald, foolish retainers of the king of Naples, whose ignorance, knavery, and stupidity represent the coarser attributes of those great, unenlightened masses which, in all communities, threaten authority by their conjunction with brute force and savage ferocity; and only under the wholesome restraint of a wise discipline can be gradually admonished into the salutary subserviency necessary for their civilization.—Ascending by degrees in the scale, the next group is that of the cunning, cruel, selfish, treacherous worldlings,—Princes and Potentates,—the peers, in outward circumstances of high birth and breeding, of the noble Prospero, whose villainous policy (not unaided by his own dereliction of his duties as a governor in the pursuit of his pleasure as a philosopher) triumphs over his fortune, and, through a devilish ability and craft, for a time gets the better of truth and virtue in his person.—From these, who represent the baser intellectual, as the former do the baser sensual, properties of humanity, we approach by a most harmonious, moral transition, through the agency of the skilfully interposed figure of the kindly gentleman, Gonzalo, those charming types of youth and love,—Ferdinand and Miranda.—The fervent, chivalrous devotion of the youth, and the yielding simplicity and sweetness of the girl, are lovely representations of those natural emotions of tender sentiments and passionate desire which, watched and guided and guarded by the affectionate solicitude and paternal prudence of Prospero, are pruned of their lavish luxuriance, and supported in their violent weakness by the wise will that teaches forbearance and self-control as the only price at which these exquisite flowers of existence may unfold their blossoms in prosperous beauty and bear their rightful harvest of happiness as well as pleasure.—Next in this wonderful gamut of being, governed by the sovereign soul of Prospero, come the shining figures of the Masque,—beautiful bright apparitions, fitly indicating the air, the fire, and all the more smiling aspects and subtler forces of nature. These minister with prompt obedience to the magical behests of science, and, when not toiling in appointed service for their great task-master, recreate and refresh his senses and his spirit with the ever-varying pageant of this beautiful Universe.—Last— highest of all—crowning with a fitful flame of lambent brightness this poetical pyramid of existence, flickers and flashes the beautiful Demon, without whose exquisite companionship we never think of the royal magician with his grave countenance of command.—Ariel seems to me to represent the keenest perceiving intellect, separate from all moral consciousness and sense of responsibility. His power and knowledge are in some respects greater than those of his master, —he can do what Prospero cannot,—he lashes up the tempest round the island,—he saves the king and his companions from shipwreck, —he defeats the conspiracy of Sebastian and Antonio, and discovers the clumsy plot of the beast Caliban,—he wields immediate influence over the elements, and comprehends alike without indignation or sympathy,—which are moral results,—the sin and suffering of humanity. Therefore,—because he is only a spirit of knowledge, he is subject to the spirit of love,—and the wild, subtle, keen, beautiful, powerful creature is compelled to serve with mutinous waywardness and unwilling subjection the human soul that pitied and rescued it from its harsher slavery to sin,—and which, though controlling it with a wise severity to the fulfilment of its duties, yearns after it with the tearful eyes of tender human love when its wild wings flash away into its newly recovered realm of lawless liberty."

OUTLINE OF SHAKESPEARE'S PROSODY.

§ 1. **Blank Verse.**—The governing element of verse structure in English is different from that in Latin and Greek. In the classical languages *quantity* forms the basis of the prosody; in English its place is taken by *stress*. In O.E. poetry *stress* and *alliteration* had been the regulating factors; afterwards, as a general rule, alliteration disappeared, except as an ornament, and *syllabic equality* was substituted, accompanied during the M.E. period by *rhyme*. The Earl of Surrey in his translation of part of the *Æneid* abandoned rhyme; and introduced *blank verse*, a sequence of five stressed and five unstressed syllables in rising rhythm (*i.e.* with the stress on the second syllable) without rhyme. This became the normal metrical form of the Elizabethan drama, *e.g.*

For this', | be sure', | to-night' | thou shalt' | have cramps' (i. 2. 325).

But a succession of such lines, as is proved by early plays like *Gorboduc*, has a most monotonous effect, and the beauty of Elizabethan verse is largely due to its *variations* from this primary type. As Shakespeare's command over his instrument increased, he more and more indulged in such variations, so that in *The Tempest*, as one of his very last plays, there are comparatively few verses in the purely normal form.

§ 2. **Normal Variations.**—Among the variations there are several which recur regularly, and which are not to be regarded as departures from a type, but as *new types*.

(i) *Stress variation.* The classification of syllables into stressed and unstressed is not exhaustive, for there are many shades of gradation between the unstressed and the strongly stressed. Thus a *weak* or *intermediate* stress may be substituted for the normal strong stress, by placing a syllable with a very slight natural accent in a normally stressed place, *e.g.*

> [1] Put' the wild' wa'ters in' this roar', allay' them (i. 2. 2).

> And him' he play'd' it for', he needs' will be' (i. 2. 108).

This variation is very common, but it is exercised under the following limits:

(*a*) The weak stress is commonest in the *fifth foot*, *e.g.*

> Thy mo'ther was' a piece' of vir'tue, and' (i. 2. 56).

(*b*) There are never more than two weak stresses in a line.

(*c*) The two weak stresses rarely come together.

(*d*) The loss of weight (except in the fifth foot) is generally made up. Either the other syllable has also a slight stress, or one of the neighbouring feet has *two* stresses, *e.g.* in the line quoted above.

> Put' the wild' wa'ters in' this roar', allay' them.

(ii) *Stress inversion.* The alternate order of stress and non-stress may be within limits *inverted*, thus changing the rhythm, for that foot, from rising to falling. As this causes two stresses to come together, and as these can only be pronounced in succession when a slight pause intervenes, this inversion commonly coincides with a pause in the sense. Hence

---

[1] A strongly stressed syllable is marked (') *e.g. wa'ters*; a lightly stressed is marked (') *e.g. in'*.

(*a*) It is commonest in the first, and, after that, in the third and fourth feet, *e.g.*

> Like' a | good' par' | ent, did' | beget' | of him' (i. 2. 94).
>
> Lie there', | my art'. | Wipe' thou | thine eyes'; | have com'fort
> (i. 2. 25).
>
> Bore' us | some leagues' | to sea'; | where' they | prepared'
> (i. 2. 145).

(*b*) It is unusual in the second foot, *e.g.*

> 'Farewell', | bro'ther!'— | We split', | we split', | we split'! (i. 1. 56).

(*c*) It is very rare in the fifth foot.

> Of Syc' | or'ax, | toads', bee' | tles, bats' | light' on | you! (i. 2. 340).

(*d*) There are never more than two inversions in a line, and we rarely find two inversions together, and never three.

Instead of a change from rising to falling rhythm, we often get a *spondaic* rhythm, through the two syllables of the foot having an approximately equal stress.

> The fresh' | springs', brine' | -pits' barr' | en place' | and fer' | tile
> (i. 2. 338).

(iii) *Omission of syllables.* An *unstressed* syllable is sometimes omitted. This happens especially after a marked pause, thus either in the first foot, or after an emphatic monosyllable, often an imperative :

> Good' | my lord', | give' me | thy fav' | our still' (iv. 1. 201).
>
> *Mir.* O', | good sir', | I do'. |
> *Pros.*   I pray' | thee, mark' | me (i. 2. 88).

(iv) *Extra syllables.* An additional unstressed syllable may be inserted anywhere in a line. It is commonest immediately before a pause, and so is most frequently found at the end of a line. These *feminine* endings, as they are sometimes called, were increasingly used by Shakespeare throughout his career, and they are most frequent in *The Tempest*, where they amount to 35 per cent. In the hands of Fletcher this species of verse "tended to exclude the simpler type altogether". The first complete blank-verse line in *The Tempest* is in this form.

> The king' | and prince' | at pray' | ers! let 's' | assist' | them (i. 1. 48).

and numerous instances may be found on every page.

Within the line the extra syllable usually comes after the *cæsura, e.g.*

> Obey' | and be' | atten' | tive. Canst thou' | rememb' | er (i. 2. 38).

Occasionally there are *two* extra syllables, but, as a rule, in lines which have this appearance, the last syllable but one is almost entirely slurred, *e.g.*

Was duke | dom large | enough: | of temp | oral roy | alties (i. 2. 110).

Many of the lines ending with proper names, *e.g.* Ferdinand, Prospero, Antonio, seem to have two extra syllables, but in these cases the penultimate syllable is slurred.

(v) *Rhyme.* Apart from the Masque, the songs, and the Epilogue, rhyme is not found in *The Tempest*, except in the couplet with which Ariel closes Act ii. 1.

§ 3. **Less-usual Variations.** — (i) *Omission of stresses.* Occasionally one of the five stresses, sometimes a whole foot, is omitted in consequence of a pause, *e.g.*

Point to | rich ends. | ⌣ — | This my mean task (iii. 1. 4).

Here the time that would be taken by the pronunciation of the omitted foot is filled up by some action of Ferdinand, such as lifting a log.

So also in the following passage (ii. 1. 218–221):

> *Seb.*   Prithee, say on:
> The setting of thine eye and cheek proclaim
> A matter from thee, and a birth indeed
> Which throes thee much to yield. |
> *Ant.* | — ⌣ | Thus, sir |

Here the foot omitted in l. 221 is supplied by a pause caused by Antonio's momentary hesitation before unfolding his plan.

These lines, which are irregular specimens of the ordinary iambic, are to be carefully distinguished from the *short lines* of from one to four feet, which are interspersed among the five-foot verses. (*a*) Occasionally in the later plays they are "imbedded" in the midst of an otherwise normal passage, *e.g.*,

> Thou dost, and think'st it much to tread the ooze
> Of the salt deep,
> To run upon the sharp wind of the north (i. 2. 252–254);

and

> And are upon the Mediterranean flote,
> Bound sadly home for Naples,
> Supposing that they saw the king's ship wreck'd
>   (i. 2. 234–236).

(*b*) Frequently they are used, especially at the end of a speech, to give emphasis to declarations:

> And deeper than did ever plummet sound
> I 'll drown my book (v. 1. 56, 57);

and
> quickly, spirit;
> Thou shalt ere long be free (v. 1. 86, 87).

(c) They are used for *exclamatory* purposes.

Thus we have *exclamations*: "All lost! to prayers, to prayers! all lost!" (i. 1. 46); "Marvellous sweet music!" (iii. 3. 19).

Addresses. "Ay, sir" (i. 2. 268).

Orders. "Approach, my Ariel, come" (i. 2. 188). "Come, thou tortoise! when?" (i. 2. 316). "No tongue! all eyes! be silent" (iv. 1. 59).

(d) They occur frequently through some *interruption* of the dialogue. Thus a line may be left incomplete because the following speaker *has not heard it*, *e.g.*:

> *Gon.*   Now, good angels
> Preserve the king.   [*They wake.*
> *Alon.* Why, how now? ho, awake! Why are you drawn?
> (ii. 1. 296–298);

or converses with a different person than the first speaker, *e.g.*:

> *Ari.* [*To Prospero*] I . . . return
> Or ere your pulse twice beat.
> *Gon.* All torment, trouble, wonder and amazement (v. 1. 102–104);

or interrupts the first speaker:

> *Seb.* But, for your conscience?
> *Ant.* Ay, sir; where lies that? if 't were a kibe (ii. 1. 265, 266).

(ii) *Extra stresses.* Conversely there are lines with six stresses. These in *The Tempest* have generally a pause after the third foot, and are divided between two speakers, *e.g.*:

> *Mir.* And yours | it is | against. |
> *Pros.*   Poor worm, | thou art | infect | ed!
> (iii. 1. 31);

and

> *Alon.* And with | him there | lie mud | ded.
> *Seb.*   But one | fiend at | a time.
> (iii. 3. 102).

§ 4. **Apparent Variations.** In addition to the real variations from the normal type of blank verse there are a number of *apparent* variations, due to differences of pronunciation between modern and Elizabethan English. These may be divided into *Accentual* and *Syllabic*.

(i) *Accentual Variations.* There has been little change of accentuation in *simple* words, but in many *compounds* and *derivatives* the accent in E.E. could be shifted from one syllable to another.

Germanic Words. Here "the fluctuations arose from the *compound* or *derivative* being felt, now as a single word (with accent usually on the first syllable), now as a group of words, with accent on the most *important*, which was usually not the first".

Thus we have such varying stresses as mid'night (i. 2. 228), and midnight' (i. 2. 128). So in pronominal, adverbial, and prepositional compounds: without' (v. 1. 271), with'out (v. 1. 179); in'to (iii. 1. 41), into' (i. 2. 191); where'fore (iii. 1. 76), wherefore' (ii. 1. 299).

In the case of derivatives, *e.g.* verbs, the stress is generally on the root-word, not the prefix, *e.g.* outdare', forgive', believe'; but be'lieve (iii. 3. 24), be'come (v. 1. 19).

Romance Words. In the M.E. period there was a struggle between the Romance and the English system of accentuation, ending in the triumph of the latter, which threw the accent on the first syllable. But in Mod.E. the influence of Latin has often restored the original accent. Shakespeare's tendency is to accent on the first syllable, but his practice is far from uniform. Thus we find: u'tensils (iii. 2. 91); con'tract (iv. 1. 84), but contract' (ii. 1. 145); sup'portable (v. 1. 145), but impor'tune (ii. 1. 122) and oppor'tune (iv. 1. 26).

(ii) *Syllabic Variations.* There are three principal cases of syllabic variations: (1) vowel + consonant, (2) vowel + vowel-like (i.e. *l, m, n, r*), (3) vowel + vowel.

(1) *Vowel and Consonant.*

A vowel may be lost before a consonant.

(*a*) *At the beginning of a word.*

This especially affected prefixes, e.g. *'bout* for *about* (i. 2. 220); *'gins* for *begins* (iii. 3. 106). In v. 1. 7: "How fares | the king | and 's follow | ers? (Con)fined | together", the prefix in *confined*, though written, seems scarcely intended to be pronounced.

The initial vowel is also very commonly lost in unemphatic monosyllables, especially *it*, e.g. *'tis* (i. 2. 185), *be't* (i. 2. 190).

(*b*) *At the end of a word.*

This belongs chiefly to Shakespeare's later plays, and is especially found in *the*, e.g.:

> Go make thyself like a nymph o' th' sea (i. 2. 301).

> But that the sea, mounting to th' welkin's cheek (i. 2. 4).

(*c*) *Within a word.*

The unaccented *e* of the verb and noun inflexions was in

the sixteenth century gradually becoming suppressed, where
no sibilant preceded.   *-es* (3rd pers. sing.) is always mute, and
-es (plural and gen. sing.) is only occasionally pronounced in
some of the earlier plays.   Even after a sibilant the *-es* of the
plural and of the gen. sing. is often not pronounced, and is
occasionally not written.

Letters | should not | be known; | *rich*(es), pov | erty | (ii. 1. 144).

The fresh | springs, brine- | pits, bar | ren *place* | and fer | tile (i. 2. 338).

Than oth | er *prin* | *cess*(es) can | that have | more time (i. 2. 170).

On the other hand, *-es* is sounded in *aches* (see note on i. 2. 370).
    -est (2nd sing.) and *-eth* (3rd sing.) are practically always
contracted in the later plays, *e.g.*:

Shrug'st thou, malice?
If thou neglect'st or dost unwillingly (i. 2. 367, 368).

-est in the superlative is often retained, but it is six times
contracted in *The Tempest*.
    -ed (past tense and part.) shows much variety, but the con-
tracted form is the commoner.
    (*d*) *In the last but one syllable.*   An unaccented vowel is
sometimes lost before a consonant in the middle of a word of
more than two syllables, *e.g.* diligent[1] (iii. 1. 42), busịness
(i. 2. 255).
    (2) *Vowel and Vowel-like.*   The letters *l, m, n,* and *r* have
been given the name of 'vowel-likes', because they can exercise the double function of a vowel or a consonant.
    (*a*) Thus one of these letters *by passing from its consonant
to its vowel value may form a new syllable.*   This is much
commoner in earlier than in later plays, *e.g.*:

They vanish'd strangelọy.[2]   No matter, since (iii. 3. 40).

    (*b*) *By passing from its vowel to its consonant value the*
'*vowel-like*' *may cause the loss of a syllable,* e.g.:
brother and yours (v. 1. 12), (brothẹ | r-and); mis'shapen
knave (v. 1. 268), (mis-shapẹ-n(kn)ave); officer and (i. 2. 84),
(off-icẹ-r-and).
    Similarly within a word the unaccented vowel often suffers
syncope before or after a 'vowel-like', *e.g.* paṛallel (i. 2. 74),
and popular (i. 2. 92).
    '*Vowel-likes*' *underwent a still further reduction analogous*

---

[1] A dot under any letter (ị) indicates that it is suppressed or slurred.
[2] A circle under a 'vowel-like' (ḷ) denotes that it has *syllabic* value.

to the suppression or slurring of vowels. Thus ḷ or ṛ could be partially suppressed before a consonant, *e.g.,* i. 2. 304:

> And hith | (er) come in't: | go, hence | with dil | igence!

(*c*) *The 'vowel-like'* r *often caused a preceding long vowel to become a diphthong out of which two syllables were developed.* Thus *fairly spoke* (iv. 1. 31); präyers (i. 1. 46); hour = ow-ər (v. 1. 4).

(3) *Vowel and Vowel.*

Two adjacent vowels may be run into one in the same or in different words.

(*a*) *In different words.*

This happens especially when the first word is *the* or *to*, e.g. th' *event* (i. 2. 117), th' afternoon (iii. 2. 83). Here the final vowel is altogether suppressed, but other final vowels rather formed a diphthong with the initial vowel, *e.g.* How came we ashore? (i. 2. 158).

(*b*) *In the same word.*

This is most frequent when the first vowel is *i* and *u*, which readily pass into *y* or *w*, e.g. consciences (ii. 1. 268); odious (iii. 1. 5). When a stressed vowel is followed by an unstressed the two may have the value of one syllable, *e.g.* being (i. 2. 72), deity (ii. 1. 268).

(*c*) *Contraction of vowels sometimes accompanies the loss of an intervening consonant.*

Thus *even* in its adverbial sense is a monosyllable in 85 cases out of 100, and is often spelt *e'en.* (But the adjective *even* is always two syllables.) So *ever* and *never* are often one syllable, and *over* is so in more than 60 per cent cases. *Whether, rather, other,* and *whither* are also often monosyllables.

GLOSSARY

abysm (i. 2. 50), abyss < O.F. *abisme, abime* < late Lat. *abyssimus*, a superl. of *abyssus*; lit. 'the profoundest depth'.

amain (iv. 1. 74), at full speed, swiftly. The word literally means 'in strength'—*a=on* or *in*, and *main* = strength < O. E. *mægen*. "Apparently not preceded by an earlier full *on main*, but formed in sixteenth century after words in *a-*, as afoot" (Murray).

amazement (i. 2. 14), confusion, distress of mind; stronger than mere astonishment. So **amazedly** in stage-direction (v. 1. 216) means 'in a state of bewilderment'. M.E. *amase*, which had often the sense of producing disaster as well as confusion. Cf. *Richard II.*, i. 3. 81, "amazing thunder".

attached (iii. 3. 5), seized, attacked by. O.F. *atachier*, from a root probably cognate with English *tack*; hence probably='to tack to'.

bat-fowling (ii. 1. 176). See note.

betid (i. 2. 31), happened. M.E. *be-tiden*, 'happen', a synonym of *tiden* < O.E. *tíd-an*, happen.

blow (iii. 1. 63), to deposit eggs on, foul, sully. Cf. *Love's Labour's Lost*, v. 2. 408, 409:

> "these summer flies
> Have blown me full of maggot ostentation".

bombard (ii. 2. 21). See note.

bootless (i. 2. 35), profitless, useless. O.E. *bót*, advantage, profit. The substantive 'boot' is used by Shakespeare in *Richard II.*, i.

i. 164: "there is no boot", *i.e.* there is no help or use.

bosky (iv. 1. 81), woody < Mid. Lat. *boscus*, a wood. Cf. *Comus*, 313, "every bosky bower".

brave (i. 2. 6; i. 2. 206), fine. F. *brave*, "brave, gay, fine, proud, braggard, valiant" (Cotgrave).

butt (i. 2. 146). See note.

candied (ii. 1. 269), congealed, crystallized (see note). Pers. *qand*, sugar, Skt. *khándava*, sweetmeats.

cat o' mountain (iv. 1. 256). "Probably one of the smaller varieties of the leopard, and the name was apparently not strictly confined to one animal" (Wright). Thus Topsell gives it as a synonym for a leopard, Minsheu for a wild cat, and Florio for an ounce.

catch (iii. 2. 111), a part-song. "Catch, round, or roundelay, and canon in unison are, in music, nearly the same thing. In all, the harmony is to be sung by several persons, and is so contrived that, though each sings precisely the same notes as his fellows, yet by beginning at stated periods of time from each other, there results a harmony of as many parts as there are singers. The catch differs only in that the words of one part are made to answer or *catch* the other, as 'Ah! how Sophia' sung like 'a house o' fire'." (Chappell, *Popular Music of the Olden Time*), quoted by Wright.

certes (iii. 3. 30), certainly. O.F. *certes*, more fully, (according to

Littré,) a certes < prob. late pop. Lat. a certis, on certain grounds.

chanticleer (i. 2. 384), the cock. Originally a proper name; O.F. *chantecler*, the name of the cock in the O.F. romance, *Reynard the Fox*. It means 'the clear singer' < *chanter*, to sing, and *cler*, clear.

chirurgeonly (ii. 1. 134), like a surgeon. Chirurgeon is the old spelling of surgeon. F. *chirurgien* < Gk. χειρουργός, a worker with the hands.

chough (ii. 1. 256), red-legged crow. Cognate with O.E. *ceó*; named from *cawing*.

cockerel (ii. 1. 30), a young cock, applied satirically to a young man. A diminutive of *cock*; perhaps of Anglo-Fr. origin, but no such word found in O.F. dictionaries; perhaps of English formation; the termination seems to be the same as in *haggerel, mongrel, pickerel*. (See Murray.)

coil (i. 2. 207), confusion, uproar. Gaelic *goil*, rage, battle.

complexion (i. 1. 27), constitution < Lat. *complexionem*. It referred in M.E. "to the four Humours mixed in varying proportions in each human body; so Chaucer, 'of his complexion he was sanguin'. Thence it denoted as now (2) the outer appearance of the face as an index of temperament, and then (3) outer appearance in general. All three meanings are common in Shakespeare" (Herford).

control (i. 2. 438), contradict, confute; the original meaning to 'check', 'verify' < O.F. *contre-role*, a duplicate register used to verify the official or first made roll.

corollary (iv. 1. 57), a supernumerary. O.F. *corolaire*, "a corollarie; a surplusage, overplus, addition to, vantage above measure" (Cotgrave) < Lat. *corollarium*, a present of a garland, a gratuity.

crab (ii. 2. 154), crab-apple. Skeat suggests that the word is perhaps allied to *crab*, the shellfish, *i.e.* pinching, sharp, sour.

decked (i. 2. 155). See note.

dew-lapped (iii. 3. 45), with a piece of loose skin hanging from the throat. The second element is O.E. *lappa*, pendulous piece, lappet, lobe; the first is uncertain.

doit (ii. 2. 30). See note.

dowle (iii. 3. 65). See note.

drollery (iii. 3. 21). See note.

ecstasy (iii. 3. 108), commotion of mind. Used in E.E. of any mental disturbance, whether due to joy, grief, or any other cause. O.F. *ecstase*, through the Latin, from Gk. ἔκστασις, displacement.

eye (ii. 1. 52). See note.

feater (ii. 1. 263), more gracefully; **featly** (i. 2. 379), nimbly, gracefully.

flat-long (ii. 1. 172), with the flat side. There were some adverbs in O.E., originally dative feminine singular, ending in *inga, unga, linga, lunga*. A few of these, without the dative suffix, exist under the form *ling* or *long*, as *headlong, sidelong, darkling, flatling*, and *flatlong*. The last two words were specially used of a blow with the flat of a sword; cf. Spenser, *Faerie Queene*, v. 5. 18: "Tho' with her sword on him she flatling strooke", and Sidney's *Arcadia*, in the description of Pamela's execution, "The pittilesse sword had such pittie of so precious an object that at first it did but hit flatlong".

flote (i. 2. 234), sea < O.E. *flot*, cf. Germ. *fluth*.

foison (ii. 1. 157; iv. 1. 110), plenty. O.F. *foison* < Lat. *fusionem*.

foundered (iv. 1. 30). See note.

frippery (iv. 1. 221), an old-clothes shop. Cotgrave translates O.F. *friperie* as "a friperie, broker's shop, street of brokers or of fripiers", and he defines *fripier* as "a mender or trimmer up of old garments, and a seller of them so mended"<O.F. *fripper*, to rub up and down, to wear to rags.

gaberdine (ii. 2. 36), a long frock of coarse material. Extended from Span. *gaban*, a great coat with a hood.

genius (iv. 1. 27). See note.

gilded (v. 1. 280). See note.

hests (i. 2. 274), commands < O.E. *hæs*, command. The final *t* is excrescent, as in *whils-t, amongs-t.*

holp (i. 2. 63), helped. Curtailed from *holpen*, p. part. of O.E. *helpan.*

inch-meal (ii. 2. 3), by inches. Compounded of inch < O.E. *ynce*, with mutation from Lat. *uncia*, and meal < O.E. *mælum*, dat. plu. of *mæl*, piece. Cf. piece-meal.

inherit (iv. 1. 154), possess < O.F. *enheriter* < Lat. *hereditare*, 'to become heir to'. It often has the sense of 'possess' in poetry in E.E. by transfer from an act to its *sequel.*

kibe (ii. 1. 266), chilblain. Welsh *cibwst = cib-gwst*, compounded from *cib*, a cup, and *gwst*, a humour, malady; hence a 'cup-like malady', from the rounded form. The English word has preserved only the syllable *cib*, rejecting the latter syllable (Skeat).

lakin (iii. 3. 1). See note.

lieu (i. 2. 123), literally 'place < Lat. *locum*. Hence *in lieu of*= 'in place of', 'instead of', and thus 'in return for'.

main-course (i. 1. 32). See note.

manage (i. 2. 70), management. Originally, like its immediate source, O.F. *manège*, a technical term for the management of horses.

Cf. *1 Henry IV.*, ii. 3. 52: "Speak terms of manage to thy bounding steed".

mantle (v. 1. 67), *cover with a scum*; cf. 'filthy-**mantled** pool' (iv. 1. 182). The verb is formed from the subs. *mantle*, a cloak or covering; M. E. *mantel*, O. F. *mantel* < Lat. *mantellum*, a napkin or covering.

marmoset (ii. 2. 157), a small American monkey. The name, however, is older than the discovery of America, as Maundeville mentions "apes, marmozettes, babewynes". O. F. *marmoset*, translated by Cotgrave, "the cock of a cistern or fountain, any antick image from whose teats water trilleth, any puppet or antick". "Thus it meant a grotesque creature, orig. a grotesque ornament on a fountain. Formed by a Parisian change of *r* to *s*, as in *chaise* for *chaire* (a chair), from Low Lat. *marmoretum*, a thing made in marble, applied to fountains. At the same time, the transference in sense from 'drinking-fountain' to 'ape' was certainly helped on by confusion with F. *marmot*, a marmoset or little monkey" (Skeat).

meddle (i. 2. 22), mix, mingle. M.E. *medlen*, O.F. *medler* < Low Lat. *misculare*, Lat. *miscere.*

merely (i. 1. 50), entirely, absolutely < Lat. *merus*, pure.

minion (iv. 1. 98), favourite. < F. *mignon*, dainty, pleasing, kind. Same root as O. H. G. *minna*, 'memory', 'love', whence *minnesinger*=singer of love.

moe (ii. 1. 127), more. "M.E. *ma*, *mo*, O.E. *má*, *mæ*, to *mára*, 'greater'; used (1) as a neut.subst., (2) as adv. The former usage, in which it was often coupled with a partitive gen., as '*ma manna*, a greater number of men', *i.e.* 'more men', led to the E.E. use, in which it was treated as the comp. of *many*, while *more* remained the comp. of *much*" (Herford).

moon-calf (ii. 2. 100), an abortion, a monstrosity, a person or conception influenced by the moon.

mow (ii. 2. 9), make grimaces. F. *moue*, a mouth, a pouting face. O. Du. *mouwe*, the protruded underlip in making a grimace.

murrain (iii. 2. 76), a plague. M. E. *moreine*, allied to O. F. *morine*, a carcass of a beast < O.F. *morir*, to die < Lat. *mori*.

nerves (i. 2. 483), sinews, muscles. This is the usual sense of the word in E.E., whereas *sinew* in E.E. often corresponds with Md.E. *nerve* < Lat. *nervum*.

ninny (iii. 2. 60), simpleton < Ital. *ninno*, a child.

nonpareil (iii. 2. 95), a matchless creature. The adj. used as subs. F. *non* = not, and *pareil* = like.

owes (i. 2. 406), owns, possesses. O. E. *ág*, *áh*, 'possess'. The modern sense arises from the notion of *obligation*, regarded as attaching to a man, like a possession.

pard (iv. 1. 256), panther.

passion (i. 2. 391; iv. 1. 143), strong emotion of any kind. The word is not confined in E.E. to its modern sense of 'anger', but, like the Lat. *passio* and Gk. πάθος, is used for the 'suffering' of any vehement feeling.

patch (iii. 2. 60), paltry fellow, fool. Probably a nickname derived from the fool's *patch*-like or motley dress. Cf. *Midsummer-Night's Dream*, iv. 1. 215: "man is but a *patched* fool." Wright, however, connects it with Italian *pazzo*, 'a fool' or 'idiot'.

pertly (iv. 1. 58), briskly. *Pert* in M.E. is another form of *perk* (adj.), smart; but in some cases it is short for *apert*, as in F. *mal-apert*, from Lat. *male + apertus*,

'too open or ready'. The two words became confused, hence the modern meaning 'forward, impudent'.

pied (iii. 2. 60), parti-coloured. Used of Trinculo because of the motley dress which he wore as jester. < *Pie*, a magpie, Lat. *pica*.

pioned (iv. 1. 64). See note.

Poor-John (ii. 2. 26), hake, salted, and dried.

premises (i. 2. 123), conditions previously made. O.F. *premisse*, < Lat. *praemissa* (sententia being understood), 'a condition sent or stated beforehand'.

prevent (i. 2. 350), forestall, and so interfere with. In E.E the original meaning of the word. 'anticipation', rather than 'interference', is generally predominant. < O.F. *prevenir*, to come before.

prime (i. 2. 72), first, chief. < Lat. *primus*.

quaint (i. 2. 317), trim, fine. dainty. O. F. *coint* < Lat. *cognitus*, 'well-known'. Used originally = 'knowing', 'prudent'. A. W. Verity quotes in illustration from Hampole's *Psalter*, Ps. crix. 98: "Aboven myn enmys quaynt thou me made", where the A.V. has *wiser*. But later F. *coint*, being wrongly supposed to come from Lat. *comptus*, 'adorned', got the sense 'trim'. This influenced English 'quaint' which got the same sense, in which it is always used by Shakespeare.

rack (iv. 1. 157). See note.

rate (i. 2. 92; ii. 1. 103), estimation. < Lat. *ratus*, p. part. of *reor*, I think, deem.

renown (v. i. 193), report. M.E. *renoun* or *renommee*, F. *renommé* < Lat. *re*, again, and *nomen*, name.

roarers (i. 1. 16). See note.

sack (ii. 2. 110), a Spanish white wine. Probably a corruption of

F. *sec*, 'dry'. In a Worcester MSS. for 1592 it is spelt *seck*. In a French version of a proclamation for regulating the prices of wine, 1633, 'sacks' is translated *vins secs*.

sans (i. 2. 97), without. A French word borrowed in fourteenth century, and originally used in French phrases only, *e.g. sans doute*; but used in E.E. in combination with English words, *e.g. As You Like It*, ii. 7. 166: "Sans teeth, sans eyes, sans taste, sans everything".

scamels (ii. 2. 159). See note.

scandal'd (iv. 1. 90), scandalous; pass. form with active meaning. < Lat. *scandalum*, Gk. σκάνδαλον, stumbling-block, offence, scandal.

signories (i. 2. 71), states of N. Italy, under the government of single princes, originally owing feudal obedience to the Holy Roman Empire. It. *signoria*, lordship, government < Lat. *senior*, older, superior.

sot (iii. 2. 88), fool. O.F. *sot*. Among the equivalents given for this by Cotgrave are: "asse, dunce, dullard, blockhead, loggerhead, groutnoll, iobernoll, grouthead, ioulthead".

stale (iv. 1. 187), a decoy, a snare. < O.E. *stalu*, theft.

stover (iv. 1. 63). See note.

swabber (ii. 2. 44), one who sweeps the deck with a swab or mop. Connected with Dutch, *zwabberen*, to drudge.

taborer (iii. 2. 145), drummer. A tabor is a small side drum generally associated with the fife. < Arabic, *tabl*, a drum.

tackle (i. 2. 147), ropes. M.E. *takel*. The suffix -*el* denotes the

agent; thus *takel* is that which *takes* or grasps, from its holding the masts firmly.

teen (i. 2. 64), sorrow. M.E. *tene*, O.E. *teóna*, accusation, vexation.

tell (ii. 1. 15), count. < O.E. *tellan*.

trash (i. 2. 81). See note.

trice (v. 1. 238), a moment. Spanish *en un tris*; from *tris*, the noise made by the cracking of glass, a crack, an instant.

troll (iii. 2. 111), roll off the tongue, sing; derivation uncertain. Connected apparently with O.F. *troller*, which Cotgrave explains by "hounds to *trowle*, ravage, or hunt out of order". Skeat therefore defines "troll a catch", to sing it irregularly.

try (i. 1. 32). See note.

twilled (iv. 1. 64). See note.

twink (iv. 1. 43), the twinkling of an eye. M.E. *twinken*, to blink, wink.

urchin (i. 2. 326). See note.

vouched (ii. 1. 57), warranted. O.F. *voucher*, to vouch, cite, pray in aid in a suit. < Lat. *vocare*, to call upon.

welkin (i. 2. 4), sky, properly a plural word = 'clouds'. Cf. M.E. *welken* = O.E. *wolcnu*, 'clouds', plural of *wolcen*, 'a cloud'. Cf. Germ. *wolke*.

wezand (iii. 2. 86), windpipe. O.E. *wǽsend*.

whist (i. 2. 378). See note.

yare (i. 1. 6), ready, quick; **yarely** (i. 1. 3), quickly, nimbly. M.E. *zare*, O.E. *geáro*, ready.

INDEX OF WORDS

GENERAL INDEX

SHAKESPEARE'S STAGE IN ITS
BEARING UPON HIS DRAMA.

§ 1. The structure and arrangements of the Elizabethan theatre are still under discussion, and many points of detail remain unsettled. The last twenty years have produced a very extensive and highly technical literature on the subject, chiefly in England, America, and Germany. It is based especially on the new evidence derived from (1) the original stage directions, (2) contemporary illustrations and descriptions. The following summary gives the conclusions which at present appear most reasonable, neglecting much speculative matter of great interest.

§ 2. When Shakespeare arrived in London, soon after 1585, theatrical exhibitions were given there in (1) public theatres, (2) private theatres, (3) the halls of the royal palaces, and of the Inns of Court.

Of the 'public' theatres there were at least three: The Theater, the Curtain, both in Shoreditch, and Newington Butts on the Bankside or Southwark shore. About 1587, the Rose, also on the Bankside, was added. All these were occasionally used by Shakespeare's company before 1599, when their headquarters became the newly built Globe, likewise on the Bankside. Of the 'private' theatres the principal, and the oldest, was the Blackfriar, on the site of the present *Times* office. It was also the property of the company in which Shakespeare acquired a share, but being let out during practically his whole career, does not count in the present connexion. At court, on the other hand, his company played repeatedly. But his plays were written for the 'public' theatre, and this alone had any influence in his stage-craft.

§ 3. The 'public' theatre differed from the other two types chiefly in being (1) dependent on daylight, (2) open overhead, and (3) partially seatless; and from the court-stages also, in (4) not using painted scenes. While they, again, had the rectangular form, the typical 'public' theatre was a round or octagonal edifice, modelled partly on the inn-yards where companies of players had been accustomed to perform, prior to the inhibition of 1574, on movable stages; partly on the arenas used for bear-baiting and cock-fighting;—sports still carried on in the 'theatres', and in part dictating their arrangements.

The circular inner area, known thence as the 'cock-pit', or 'pit', had accordingly no seats; admission to it cost one penny (6d. in modern money), and the throng of standing spectators were known as the 'groundlings'. More expensive places (up to 2s. 6d.) with seats, were provided in tiers of galleries which ran round the area, one above the other, as in modern theatres; the uppermost being covered with a thatched roof.

§ 4. The Stage (using the term to describe the entire scenic apparatus of the theatre) included (1) the *outer stage*, a rectangular platform (as much as 42 feet wide in the largest examples) projecting into the circular area, from the back wall, and thus surrounded by 'groundlings' on three sides. Above it were a thatched roof and hangings but no side or front curtains. In the floor was a trap-door by which ghosts and others ascended or descended. At the back were (2) two projecting wings, each with a door opening obliquely on to the stage, the *recess* between them, of uncertain shape and extent, forming a kind of

i

inner stage. Above this was (3) an upper room or rooms, which included the actors' 'tiring house', with a window or windows opening on to (4) a *balcony* or gallery from which was hung (5) a *curtain*, by means of which the inner recess could be concealed or disclosed.

§ 5. The most important divergence of this type of structure from that of our theatres is in the relation between the outer stage and the auditorium. In the modern theatre the play is treated as a picture, framed in the proscenium arch, seen by the audience like any other picture from the front only, and shut off from their view at any desired moment by letting fall the curtain. An immediate consequence of this was that a scene (or act) could terminate only in one of two ways. Either the persons concerned in it walked, or were carried, off the stage; or a change of place and circumstances was *supposed* without their leaving it. Both these methods were used. The first was necessary only at the close of the play. For this reason an Elizabethan play rarely ends on a *climax* such as the close of Ibsen's *Ghosts*; the overpowering effect of which would be gravely diminished if, instead of the curtain falling upon Osvald's helpless cry for "the sun", he and his mother had to walk off the stage. Marlowe's *Faustus* ends with a real climax, because the catastrophe *ipso facto* leaves the stage clear. But the close of even the most overwhelming final scenes of Shakespeare is relatively quiet, or even, as in *Macbeth*, a little tame. The concluding lines often provide a motive for the (compulsory) clearing of the stage.

In the *Tragedies*, the dead body of the hero has usually to be borne ceremoniously away, followed by the rest; so Aufidius in *Coriolanus*: "Help, three o' the chiefest soldiers: I'll be one". Similarly in *Hamlet* and *King Lear*. In *Othello*, Desdemona's bed was apparently in the curtained recess, and at the close the curtains were drawn upon the two bodies, instead of their being as usual borne away.

The close of the *Histories* often resembles the dispersing of an informal council after a declaration of policy by the principal person ; thus *Richard II.* closes with Bolingbroke's announcement of the penance he proposes to pay for Richard's death; *Henry IV.* with his orders for the campaign against Northumberland and Glendower; *King John* with Falconbridge's great assertion of English patriotism.

In the *Comedies*, the leading persons will often withdraw to explain to one another at leisure what the audience already knows (*Winter's Tale, Tempest, Merchant of Venice*), or to carry out the wedding rites (*As You Like It, Midsummer-Night's Dream*); or they strike up a measure and thus (as in *Much Ado*) naturally dance off the stage. Sometimes the chief persons have withdrawn before the close, leaving some minor character—Puck (*Midsummer-Night's Dream*) or the Clown (*Twelfth Night*) —to wind up the whole with a snatch of song, and then retire himself.

§ 6. But the most important result of the exposed stage was that it placed strict limit upon dramatic illusion, and thus compelled the resort, for most purposes, to conventions resting on symbolism, suggestion, or make-believe. It was only in dress that anything like simulation could be attempted; and here the Elizabethan companies, as is well known, were lavish in the extreme. Painted scenes, on the other hand, even had they been available, would have been idle or worse, when perhaps a third of the audience would see, behind the actors, not the scenes but the people in the opposite gallery, or the gallants seated on the stage. Especially where complex and crowded actions were introduced, the most beggarly symbolic suggestion was cheerfully accepted. Jonson, in the spirit of classical realism, would have tabooed all such intractable matter; and he scoffed, in his famous Prologue, at the "three rusty swords" whose clashing had to do duty for "York and Lancaster's long jars". Shakespeare's realism was never of this literal kind, but in bringing Agincourt upon the stage of the newly built Globe in the following year (1599) he showed himself so far sensitive to criticisms of this type that he expressly appealed to the audience's imagination—"eke out our imperfections with your thoughts"—consenting, moreover, to assist them by the splendid descriptive passages interposed between the Acts.

It is probable that the Elizabethan popular audience did not need any such appeal. It had no experience of elaborate 'realism' on the stage; the rude movable stages on which the earliest dramas had been played compelled an ideal treatment of *space* and a symbolic treatment of *properties*; and this tradition, though slowly giving way, was still paramount throughout Shakespeare's career. Thus every audience accepted as a matter of course (1) the representation of *distant* things or places simultaneously on the stage. Sidney, in 1580, had ridiculed the Romantic plays of his time with "Asia of one side and Africa of the other", indicated by labels. But Shakespeare in 1593-4 could still represent the tents of Richard III. and Richmond within a few yards of one another, and the Ghosts speaking alternately to each. Every audience accepted (2) the presence on the stage, in full view of the audience, of accessories irrelevant to the scene in course of performance. A property requisite for one set of scenes, but out of place in another, could be simply ignored while the latter were in progress; just as the modern audience sees, but never reckons into the scenery, the footlights and the prompter's box. Large, movable objects, such as beds or chairs, were no doubt often brought in when needed; but no one was disturbed if they remained during an intervening scene in which they were out of place. And "properties either difficult to move, like a well, or so small as to be unobtrusive, were habitually left on the stage as long as they were wanted, whatever scenes intervened" (Reynolds).

Thus in Jonson's *The Case is Altered* (an early play, not yet reflecting his characteristic technique), Jaques, in III. 2, hides his gold in the earth and covers it with a heap of dung to avoid suspicion. In IV. 4, he removes the dung to assure himself that the gold is still there. The intervening scenes represent rooms in Ferneze's palace, and Juniper's shop; but the heap of dung doubtless remained on the stage all the time. Similarly in Peele's *David and Bethsabe*, the spring in which Bethsabe bathes; and in his *Old Wives' Tale*, 'a study' and a 'cross', which belong to unconnected parts of the action.

It follows from this that the *supposed locality of a scene could be changed* without any change in the properties on the stage, or even of the persons. What happened was merely that some properties which previously had no dramatic relevance, suddenly acquired it, and *vice versa*; that a tree, for instance, hitherto only a stage property out of use, became a *tree* and signified probably, a wood. The change of scene may take place without any break in the dialogue, and be only marked by the occurrence of allusions of a different tenor.

Thus in *Doctor Faustus*, at v. 1106 f., Faustus is in "a fair and pleasant green", on his way from the Emperor's Court at Wittenberg; at v. 1143 f., he is back in his house there. In *Romeo and Juliet*, I. 4. 5, Romeo and his friends are at first in the street; at I. 4, 114, according to the Folio, "they march about the stage and serving-men come forth with their napkins"; in other words, we are now in Capulet's hall, and Capulet presently enters meeting his guests. This is conventionalized in modern editions.

§ 7. **The Inner Stage.**—An audience for which the limitations of the actual stage meant so little, might be expected to dispense readily with the concessions to realism implied in providing an actual inner chamber for scenes performed ' within ', and an actual gallery for those performed ' aloft '. And the importance and number of the former class of scenes has, in fact, been greatly exaggerated.

Applying modern usages to the semi-mediæval Elizabethan stage, Brandl (*Einleitung* to his revised edition of Schlegel's translation) and Brodmeier (Dissertation on the stage conditions of the Elizabethan drama), put forward the theory of the ' alternative ' scene; according to which the inner and the outer stage were used ' alternately ', a recurring scene, with elaborate properties, being arranged in the former, and merely curtained off while intervening scenes were played on the outer, or main stage. But while this theory is plausible, as applied to some of Shakespeare's plays (e.g. the intricate transitions between rooms at Belmont and piazzas at Venice, in the *Merchant*), it breaks down in others (e.g. *Cymbeline*, II. 2, 3; *Richard II.*, I. 3, 4), and especially in many plays by other dramatists.

It is probable that the use of the ' inner stage ' was in general restricted to two classes of scene : (1) where persons ' within ' formed an integral though subordinate part of a scene of which the main issue was decided on the outer stage; as with the play-scene in *Hamlet*, or where Ferdinand and Miranda are discovered playing chess in *The Tempest*; (2) where a scene, though engaging the whole interest, is supposed to occur in an inner chamber. Thus Desdemona's chamber, Prospero's cell, Timon's cave, Lear's hovel, the Capulet's tomb.

§ 8. **The Balcony.**—There is less doubt about the use of the balcony or gallery. This was in fact an extremely favourite resource, and its existence in part explains the abundance of serenade, rope-ladder, and other upper-story scenes in Elizabethan drama.

From the balcony, or the window above it, Juliet discoursed with Romeo, and Sylvia with Proteus (*Two Gentlemen of Verona*, IV. 2); Richard III. addressed the London citizens, and the citizen of Angers the rival Kings. From the window the Pedant in *Taming of the Shrew*, V. 1, hails Petruchio and Grumio below; and Squire Tub, in Jonson's *Tale of a Tub*, I. 1, puts out his head in answer to the summons of Parson Hugh. But whole scenes were also, it is probable, occasionally enacted in this upper room. This is the most natural interpretation of the scenes in Juliet's chamber (IV. 3, 5). On the other hand, though the Senators in *Titus Andronicus*, I. 1, " go up into the ' Senate House '", it is probable that the debate later in the scene, on the main stage, is intended to be in the Senate-house by the convention described in § 6.

For further reference the following among others may be mentioned:—

G. F. Reynolds, *Some Principles of Elizabethan Staging* (*Modern Philology*, II. III.); A. Brandl, *Introduction* to his edition of Schlegel's translation of Shakespeare; V. E. Albright, *The Shakesperian Stage* (New York); W. Archer, *The Elizabethan Stage* (*Quarterly Review*, 1908); W. J. Lawrence, *The Elizabethan Playhouse and other Studies* (1st and 2nd series); D. Figgis, *Shakespeare, a study*.

From one or other of these, many of the above examples have been taken.

C. H. H.